MENDING BROKEN PIECES

VOLUME 2

FIFTY DEVOTIONALS

PEARLIE SINGH AND **DONALD SINGH**

WESTBOW
PRESS®
A DIVISION OF THOMAS NELSON
& ZONDERVAN

WestBow Press books may be ordered through booksellers or by contacting:

WestBow Press
A Division of Thomas Nelson & Zondervan
1663 Liberty Drive
Bloomington, IN 47403
www.westbowpress.com
844-714-3454

ISBN: 978-1-6642-5664-4 (sc)
ISBN: 978-1-6642-5666-8 (hc)
ISBN: 978-1-6642-5665-1 (e)

Library of Congress Control Number: 2022901787

Print information available on the last page.

WestBow Press rev. date: 05/01/2023

To our sons – Deejay and Kevin who we deeply love.
May God's favor continue to follow you.

Contents

Your Identity

Good Choices

God in the Crisis

The Battles We Face

The Winner in You

Acknowledgements

Thanks to our wonderful parents, Rosalind and Frederick Jai Mohan, Donald and Bernice Singh (deceased) for all you have deposited in our lives. Thanks to our two sons, Deejay and Kevin for initiating the idea of writing this book. We are thankful for the professors and Faculty of Queens College and LaGuardia Community College for your academic contribution and support. Thank you WestBow Press for your editing and publishing services. Most of all we are grateful that we are a part of Christian Community Fellowship Church.

Introduction

Mending Broken Pieces, as the title suggests, is about bringing hope to the weak, wounded, and unloved. The characters in this book have had to deal with various types of situations, so they aren't unfamiliar with brokenness, struggles, or blunders.

The truth is, life's not always filled with beautiful scenery, lively parties, singing, and laughter. Often we have to deal with discouragement, distress, and tense, depressing environments. Other times, life may look like a big jigsaw puzzle, with all the pieces scattered everywhere, and we have no clue whatsoever as to how it should all come together. Whatever our experiences are, God has promised to always be right there with us. In fact, this is the exact place where God loves to make himself known to us! When we allow God to handle our circumstances, something good is bound to come out from all the mess.

From a glimpse of our personal lives and also of the lives Bible characters, readers will see that God allows us to go through all kinds of storms and battles. Often this is the very platform he uses to show us how powerful, kind, loving, strong, and excellent he really is. Although we may not understand why negative circumstances happen in our lives, we do know that God has a purpose for each of them.

Throughout the Bible, many of the men and women found themselves in complex, restricted, and hopeless situations.

Consider the following: Abraham, Joseph (Jacob's son), Jacob, Moses, Elijah, Daniel, David, the apostle Paul, Peter, John, Joseph (Mary's husband), the prodigal son, Sarah, Hagar, Hannah, Naomi, Ruth, Esther, Mary, Elizabeth, the Samaritan woman. All struggled in one way or another. They were broken, shattered, troubled, depressed, anxious, fearful, concerned, disappointed, or unfulfilled. However, some brought trouble on themselves. Whatever the case, God didn't turn his back on any of the characters. He showed up—each time in a beautiful way.

In other instances, challenges brought people to a place where they questioned God or doubted his promises. Some even made huge blunders, so they found themselves having to run away from circumstances they couldn't handle. As seen in devotional fifty-one, one Bible character, Jacob, had to get away from his brother because he had stolen his brother's blessing. But his offense didn't prevent God from encountering him in a most unique way; this experience caused him to reflect on his actions, and as a result, his life took another turn. God's mercy and kindness will always transcend our wrongdoings. Instead of chiding or condemning us for our flaws and mistakes, God desires to minister to us. God is about transformation—he wants to change mindsets.

Another great insight into these readings is the way we human beings respond or react to various situations and people; this is what will determine the outcome. When we impulsively react to negative circumstances or people's comments, we can end up making wrong decisions or saying the wrong thing, but when we reflect and meditate on them, we are able to respond in a way that will bring about positive change and solutions to problems.

A response causes a chain reaction, as seen in the lives of many of the Bible characters listed above. For example, in devotionals two, three, and one hundred, both Joseph and

Ruth faced tough circumstances that could have caused them to react foolishly. Fortunately, Joseph's positive response to his brothers' cruel and unfair treatment, and the mistreatment from Potiphar, his master, brought about a significant change in history. Not only was he promoted from pit to palace, but God provided a beautiful family for him. Also, Ruth's daring move of choosing to go with Naomi, her mother-in-law, to her hometown, despite the unfavorable circumstances surrounding her life with no prospect of financial stability, resulted in a remarkable turnaround. Ruth reaped the benefits of her honorable choice. Ultimately, her friendship and loyalty to Boaz brought about a marriage God had orchestrated.

As you turn the pages of this book, you will find inspirational guidelines, scriptural teachings, and personal experiences - illustrating that God is still working in the hearts of people to bring about positive change. These readings are specially designed to show us that God is able to deliver us from sin, and they reveal how to overcome temptations, challenges, and obstacles we might face daily. As you read these devotionals, they will create an atmosphere of praise and worship in your heart, which will motivate you to trust God for your healing, deliverance, finances—as well as any concern or issue that may come your way.

Because God deeply cares about every aspect of our lives, this book, filled with fifty devotionals, will reveal to you God's plan for your life on earth. As you read them, they will transform your thinking by motivating you to think *good thoughts about yourself and God.*

Pearlie and Donald

From the Author's Desk

When many people were eager to find out how this devotional book got started, I didn't need to rack my brain to come up with the answer. I remembered the exact moment when the idea struck me. It was clear and definite. Yet it demanded a process. A passion.

Passion will drive you. It's not something you can plan or fabricate. It just happens. Spontaneously. You might not even understand where it originated, but seemingly out of the blues, you find yourself doing it. Such was my experience many years ago.

During my adolescence years, without even realizing it, I had become enthusiastic about reading the Bible, especially Psalms, the stories in the Bible, and the epistles in the New Testament. So I read the Bible, studied it, memorized it, and wrote down favorite scriptures in my notepads. Later on in my life, I took specific excerpts and chapters from the Bible and wrote about them. Most of all, I make a conscious decision to live by its principles. I now know God is the One who has been orchestrating this process all along. He had put that desire in my heart. All God has been depositing in my life during these many years has made me grow to treasure the Word of God, which has become "a lamp to my feet and a light to my path" (Psalm 119:105 NKJV).

Looking back at my life, I can say this devotional book got started from a very early age.

That Sunday afternoon was like every other day, yet it was one of the most significant moments in my life. While sitting in that Sunday school class as the teacher started to teach about God's love, something gripped my heart. That was the day I accepted Jesus as my personal Lord and Savior. I was only eleven years old, but I know I made a lifelong decision to dedicate my life to serving the Lord.

The next morning, during *my first devotional time* with the Lord, I was reading my Bible and had an experience that still resonates in my mind. I distinctly remember sitting comfortably on the floor in one of the back rooms of our house. As I was reading one of the psalms, I was so inspired that I felt droplets of tears welling up in my eyes. Then I didn't realize what was happening. I now know the Holy Spirit was doing a beautiful work in my soul and connecting me to my heavenly Father.

Over and over again, as I read the scriptures, they seem to leap off the page at me. I actually love when this happens. In troubling, discouraging, puzzling moments, and even when there seems to be silence or a standstill in my life, the Word has inspired and instructed me to such a point that it gave me insight and the know-how to deal with the pressure, discomfort, or anxiety connected with the situation.

I discover that the Word of God is powerful, enlightening, and exciting. On many occasions, the scriptures have nurtured, guided, comforted, strengthened, motivated, lifted, and cheered me. Moreover, the scriptures have given me a reason to live. According to the Bible, God has a purpose and plan for every single person. We aren't just mere human beings going through life and doing our own thing. God planned our lives beforehand so that through Christ Jesus we can walk in his ways (Eph. 2:10

NKJV). However, we can lose track of what God has really created us on this earth for—like I experienced many years ago—a period I consider the darkest time of my life.

You see, I felt I could live without God, and as a result, I lost the true purpose and reason for living. What followed was brokenness, depression, and confusion instead of joy, peace, and fulfillment I had once experienced. As I look back, I realize something beautiful came out of that bad experience; *I came face-to-face with God's grace.* When I wasn't even looking for God, he was looking for me, and like a great magnet, he drew me back into his arms—the arms of a loving heavenly Father. Because of God's great love for us, he goes before us and follows us, even in those dark, lonely, and rebellious paths, where he continues to place his hand of mercy and blessing on us. Beyond the shadow of a doubt, I now know his presence will pursue me; I can never escape God. His unfailing love will always be right there with me to strengthen, comfort, and cover me.

Over the years, from my collection of writing material—notebooks of all sizes and colors, and files on my computer—I have asked the Lord to lead me to the ones that will most bless and help people. These readings therefore not only encapsulate meaningful and treasured times we have had with the Lord but also those depressed, anxious, disappointed, and defeated moments. As the author of this book and my husband, the coauthor, we believe *Mending Broken Pieces* will captivate men, women, as well as youths; it will motivate them to encounter God's amazing love and to become aware of the enablement of God's supernatural power in them to overcome sin, temptation, and everyday challenges.

Pearlie

Your Identity

There's a deep cry within all of us human beings to be acknowledged. We want people to identify with what we are doing—our pursuits in life, our goals, our talents and skills, and even our weaknesses. We don't want to be labeled in a negative way. In fact, we want people to accept us despite our flaws. If this doesn't happen, chaos can break out, and dark shadows can infiltrate our minds.

This is the time when we need an Advocate, a heavenly Father who deeply loves us to the point that he will grace us with his presence. Actually, he will encounter our hearts in such a beautiful way that we will understand what it means to have a friend who totally identifies with us.

This friend, Jesus, will make all the difference. He is the one who will show you mercy and give you a fresh start. Then you will wear that new identity that says, "I am God's masterpiece! I am more than a conqueror. I am a champion." I am exactly the person I am supposed to be according to God's plan.

Graced with His Presence

There is now no condemnation for
those who are in Christ Jesus.
—Romans 8:1 (NIV)

Have you ever made a mistake that made you feel so horrible
that you just wanted to run far away from it or from the person
involved? Although running away never solves the problem,
people do it anyway. Some people may even find themselves
running from God. But can we really run from him?

In Genesis 27, when Jacob tricked his father, Isaac, and
stole Esau's blessing, Esau was so angry with him that Jacob
had to run away. His plan was to travel to Haran, where his
uncle lived, so he could spend some time with him while Esau
cooled off (Genesis 27:42–44).

On his way to his uncle, Jacob stopped to set up camp.
When he slept in the open air, we wonder whether Jacob was
thinking about how much he had hurt his brother or whether
his actions would backfire on him. Instead of being blessed,
would he be cursed? Whatever his thoughts were, God wanted
to get Jacob's attention. Jacob's mistake didn't prevent God
from chasing him. How many times do we think otherwise?
When we sin, we start to feel so bad that we feel like hiding

from God. That's the guilt of sin causing us to feel this way. Despite Jacob's blunder, note how God dealt with him.

Little did Jacob realize that something would happen that would forever change his life. That night as he slept, he dreamed of a stairway with angels ascending and descending from earth to heaven. He even saw the Lord standing on top of the stairway (Genesis 28:12–13). Not only did Jacob get a vision of the Lord, but he heard his voice saying, "I am with you and will watch over you wherever you go, and I will bring you back to this land. I will not leave you until I have done what I have promised you" (Genesis 28:15 NIV).

Wow! What a wonderful promise! This encounter with God must have blown Jacob's mind. Even though he was on the run for a wrong deed, God still remembered him. He had disappointed not only his brother but also his father. Yet God still graced him with his presence. Isn't this like God—to show us his gracious and merciful hand? God's greatest joy is to set people free from their wrongdoings so they can have a responsive heart toward him.

I believe Jacob needed to hear God's encouraging voice. This must have softened his heart. It's no wonder his response to God was:

> If God will be with me and will watch over me on this journey ... then the Lord will be my God and this stone that I have set up as a pillar will be God's house, and of all that you give me I will give you a tenth. (Genesis 28:20–22 NIV)

What a commitment! What a change of heart! Jacob may have never dreamed that God would pursue him this way. But God's love is relentless; he doesn't give up on us.

Have you made mistakes in the past that were condemning you? That's because you were hearing the voice of those mistakes and the devil in your head. Remember: God doesn't want to condemn you. God has started a good work in you which he wants to complete. This will happen as you yield your life to God, who "will empower you with inner strength ... As you trust in him, your roots will grow down into God's love and *keep you strong*" (Ephesians 3:16–17; emphasis added).

Now tell God the following:

Prayer

God, this is the moment I'm going to make my life right. Thank you for forgiving me for all my mistakes I have made. Today I surrender my entire life to the Holy Spirit, who will empower and strengthen me so I can now live to please you. Amen.

52

Dark Shadows in Our Minds

> You are beautiful ... as majestic as an army with
> billowing banners ... Even among ... countless young
> women, I would still choose my dove, my *perfect one.*
> —Song of Solomon 6:4, 9 (emphasis added)

The book of Song of Solomon illustrates a beautiful love
story of a man and a woman, which is a representation of
the relationship between God, our heavenly Father, and his
children. However, this woman struggles with her self-image.
She tells the other young women,

> I am dark but beautiful ... Don't stare at me
> because I am dark—the sun has darkened my
> skin. (Song of Solomon 1:5–6)

Could the way this woman views herself be the reason
for her inner conflict? What has caused her to view herself as
being dark? Has she been comparing herself with others, or
have her past disappointments and failures attributed to these
negative feelings? She has even come to the place where she is
so conscious of this darkness that she believes others are staring
at her. She points out that she is dark because her brothers

forced her to care for their vineyards, so she couldn't care for herself (Song of Solomon 1:6). When we're in such a place, we may feel that we need to make excuses for the darkness that exists in our lives. But do excuses or blaming others help us to move forward?

Clearly, this woman has to deal with feelings of self-pity and low self-esteem, but how does God view her?

In the above text, the man refers to his lover, the woman, as "my perfect one." That's exactly how God sees us—as perfect in his eyes! This concept may be difficult to comprehend because of the many weaknesses and flaws we are aware of on a continual basis. But when God says he sees us as perfect, he is actually telling us he doesn't want us to focus on the negative stuff of the past or even the present; he wants to take us to a higher and deeper spiritual walk with him.

This means it's time for positive change to take place.

In Song of Solomon 6:10, the young man notices the change that is taking place in this woman and praises her: "Who is this, arising like the dawn" As we know, at dawn, we behold a brand-new day. It's not time to remember all the wrongs and failures of the previous day or the past. It's time for a change to take place in our hearts. In other words, we need to recognize that "the faithful love of the Lord never ends … His mercies begin afresh each morning" (Lamentations 3:22–23; emphasis added). Acknowledging that God is faithful and merciful, despite our past failures and struggles, will fill us with new hope. And hope changes our outlook in life; it enables us to open up our hearts more readily to God. As we do so, the Holy Spirit will arise in our souls like a dawn. Then the dark shadows that want to linger and trail us have to flee (Song of Solomon 2:17).

What are some dark shadows that may linger in our minds? Guilt, condemnation, shame, embarrassing moments? We can carry countless negative stuff all through life. They will trail us and cause us to feel horrible, weak, and purposeless. But that's not the way God wants us to live. God has a much greater plan for our lives than what our feelings or people are telling us.

God wants to change negative mindsets.

Amid wrong or negative view of ourselves, we need to hear God's voice calling out to us, telling us we are fair, bright, beautiful, and as majestic as an army (Song of Solomon 6:4, 10). What a great way to view ourselves! In God's eyes, we are not only beautiful but also as majestic as an army. This means we need to see ourselves as strong and capable; God has equipped us to fight the powers of darkness. Therefore, we shouldn't see ourselves as being defeated by our weaknesses or sins. We are conquerors. Through the Holy Spirit, we *possess inner strength* to be victorious over every temptation that comes our way.

People may judge us by the negative lifestyle of the past. However, how do you measure your life? By the struggles or defeated moments you've had? This is a moment for us to become aware that God wants to change negative mindsets. He is now saying,

> I will give you a new heart ... I will take out your stony, stubborn heart and give you a *tender, responsive heart.* And I will put my Spirit in you so that you will follow my decrees and be careful to obey my regulations. (Ezekiel 36:26–27; emphasis added)

God wants to change hearts. Then you will have a heart that desires to please God. Even now, as you *start to rise* from defeated and depressed positions, declare the following:

Declaration

I declare that I won't allow the darkness of the past to trail me anymore. I am now empowered and equipped with inner strength because of the Holy Spirit living inside me. This means I will win the battle I have to face every day and in every situation. I don't need to stay defeated.

53

Our Advocate: The Father's Deep Love for Us

Joyful are those who listen to me, watching for me
daily at my gates, waiting for me outside my home.
—Proverbs 8:34

Through the above verse, you get the picture of a person who is passionate about someone. I think of a son who can hardly wait for his daddy to come home, so he is longingly and patiently waiting outside his house for that moment when his father would turn the corner. At the first glimpse of him, he just couldn't stand to wait on the sidewalk any longer, so he starts running toward him with such excitement that he jumps straight into his daddy's arms. This son knows his father loves him and will never let him fall and hurt himself. This epitomizes love. True affection. Trust.

This son has a deep love for his earthly father—a child who truly delights to see his father and wants to spend time with him. I'm sure his excitement captivated his father.

What kind of relationship do you have with your heavenly Father? Are you excited about him?

Through the psalmist David, we get a true quality believers in Christ should possess. In Psalm 63:1 (NIV), he declares, "O God, you are my God; earnestly I seek you; my soul thirsts for you; my body longs for you." Does this verse express how much you desire God? Is our love relationship with God marked by enthusiasm and a search for knowing his ways? What are some ways we can show our affection to God?

The writer John makes us aware of what it means to relate intimately to our heavenly Father by saying, "Those who obey God's word truly show how completely they love him. That is how we know we are living in him. Those who say they live in God should live their lives as Jesus did" (1 John 2:5–6). As believers, our lives should model obedience, love, and kindness—attributes that denote Jesus's lifestyle on earth.

John was writing to believers in Christ because he was interested in their spiritual lives. He didn't want them to fall into sin. But he reminded them that if they did fall into sin, they had an advocate who would plead their case before the Father. Jesus is the sacrifice who atones for our sins (1 John 2:1–2). His sacrifice on the cross tells us how much God cares about our spiritual lives.

Throughout life, we will face many temptations by Satan; he is the deceiver of the world, who is constantly trying to get God's people to sin. But John points out that as God's children, our sins are forgiven through Jesus Christ, and we have won the battle with the evil one (1 John 2:12—13). This means we don't need to go on sinning; Christ, who now lives in us, is greater than all the power of darkness, sin, temptations, and evil. We, therefore, have the ability through the Holy Spirit to overcome every sin and to enjoy a beautiful relationship with our heavenly Father.

What is God's plan for believers who have sinned against him? For sure, God doesn't want to condemn them. But if we do sin, we have an advocate who is pleading our case before the Father. As we decide to turn away from that sin, Jesus, who is the "atoning sacrifice for our sins," will forgive us. In this way, we will again align ourselves with the will of God. Even now, as you choose to be obedient to God, tell him the following:

Prayer

Lord, I long to have a relationship with you, where the material and temporal pleasures of this world don't matter. To obtain true joy and fulfillment, I know I need to obey your commands. Right now I entrust my entire life to your hands: my desires, family, job, dreams, and plans. Amen.

54

I Will Remain Confident

Though a mighty army surrounds me, my heart will not
be afraid. Even if I am attacked, *I will remain confident.*
—Psalm 27:3 (emphasis added)

What are some things in your life that can prevent you from
being confident? What recurring failures, people's criticisms, or
mountainous situations in your path are causing you to become
fearful?

In Psalm 27, when surrounded by a mighty army, David
declared that he was confident. Why was he not afraid? David
displayed a level of confidence that is beyond human reasoning.
This is because David's eyes weren't on the enemy who was
attacking him, but his heart was set on living in the house of
the Lord all the days of his life (Psalm 27:4). Living and serving
God were David's reasons for living—his number-one priority
and passion. What's more, David realized God was powerful
and loving and kind, so instead of thinking of all the enemies
who were trying to bring him down, he continued to praise
God, depending on him to see him through.

For David, God was his ultimate focus. He knew God would
conceal him when troubles came; God would hide him in his
sanctuary. For that reason, he was able to hold his head high

above his enemies and shout praises to his God, even before the victory was won (Psalm 27:5–6). What is our response when difficult times hit? Are your days filled with complaining and worrying or praising?

David understood that God was sovereign. He knew his concern was also God's concern. When we have this perception of God, we will believe God will take care of the situations on hand in ways beyond our understanding. That's the time when we keep our eyes on him; he will work out all the circumstances in our lives.

During this time David was also delighting in the Lord's perfections, knowing God would conceal him when troubles came his way (Psalm 27:4–5). In this case, David didn't crumble under the weight of the circumstances. He made room for God to perfect him. Can you identify with this? Have you ever been in a challenging or hostile environment and you just knew God was with you? You can feel his hand on your life. These are the moments when his anointing is so strong that you can almost feel him carrying you like a mother would carry her baby. At times, how much we need this kind of comfort!

In the middle of our circumstances, God has promised to perfect what concerns us (Psalm 138:8). Even when we feel overwhelmed by people or situations we have no control over, God still has a good plan in mind for our lives. God is always good, although at times we may feel bad. As we keep our eyes on God, we can be assured that he is walking with us—counseling us and perfecting us until the victory is won. It's a process.

God's plan for our lives is never to break us but to build us. Although we may feel like a mighty army is attacking us, the enemies won't have a chance to destroy us emotionally or spiritually. God's on our side. Like David, let's not be fearful but remain confident, knowing that "when you pass through the deep, stormy sea, *you can count on [God] to be there with you*" (Isaiah 43:2 TPT, emphasis added).

Do you believe God will conceal you and keep you safe when trouble comes your way? Because God keeps his promises, we can rely on him to be our helper and to hold us up so securely that we can actually feel him sheltering, protecting, comforting, and strengthening us. For that reason, let's hold our head up high and start shouting praises to God, knowing we have the victory.

Prayer

Lord, during this time we choose to take our eyes off the raging waves of the storm or the enemies surrounding us. We choose to keep our eyes on you. Thank you for giving us peace and strength amid this complex path we don't understand. Amen.

55

You Are Blessed with a Sound Mind

> For God has not given us a spirit of fear, but of
> power and of love and of a sound mind.
> —2 Timothy 1:7 (NKJV)

Our mind is valuable. God is very much interested in the way our minds function. We can liken our minds to an engine in a car; if the engine isn't working properly, the car won't function well. This means it will fail to serve the purpose for which it was intended. In the same way, God has created all of us for a specific purpose on earth. For that reason, he has given us a mind to think logically and make healthy decisions.

Is something preventing you from thinking clearly and making sound decisions? As we go through life, we will continuously face all kinds of situations where fear, anxiety, worry, frustration, confusion, turmoil, and pain can affect our minds to the point that we lose confidence in ourselves. It's at this point in our lives that we become vulnerable, and we start to lose control.

There is no denying that the devil knows our weak points, so he will purposely set out to target God's children. His objective is always the same—to corrupt our minds. The devil's plan is never good; he will try every technique to destroy us emotionally and spiritually by bombarding our minds with negative thoughts, such as:

- ~ Bad things will happen to you.
- ~ You aren't worth too much.
- ~ You aren't good enough.
- ~ You have too many flaws and weaknesses.
- ~ You will never overcome that weakness.
- ~ You will never make it.
- ~ You won't be able to accomplish the good things God has planned for you.
- ~ God will not answer your prayers.
- ~ You will always live in poverty.
- ~ You will never overcome your slanderous and swearing tongue.

These are all lies we need to become aware of. This is the devil's strategy to fill our minds with negativity so we can lose hope. Then we will be filled with self-doubt, uncertainty, and a lack of confidence; and we will start to question our worth and significance in this world.

The devil's number-one purpose is to deceive us and lead us astray. Thank goodness, God has a greater and better plan than his. God wants to transform the way we think. This can happen only when we start to *think good thoughts about ourselves and God.*

There was a time in my life when I lived in fear. Then I heard Joyce Meyers talking about how destructive fear is. I realize I was fearful of the future; I was afraid that bad things would happen in my life. Through her sermon, I now believe God doesn't want his people to live in fear; he wants us to overcome any negative emotion.

When we feel anxious and worried, we need to let God into

our thought lives. Through reading the scriptures, God can change the negative way we think. One beautiful verse I love to repeat and speak over my family's lives is Psalm 112:7 (KJV). "[The righteous] shall not be afraid of evil tidings: his heart is fixed, trusting in the Lord." This verse changed my mindset. Instead of fearing "evil tidings," I learned to trust God. I now envision the good things God has in store for me and my family. He has promised to hide us in the secret place of his presence (Psalm 31:19–20). This promise made me realize how much God is interested in our state of mind. Using the Word of God is the best antidote to dealing with fear.

In Luke 4, Jesus himself used the Word. Jesus was fasting for forty days, so he was extremely hungry, which the devil was aware of (Luke 4:1–2). Knowing Jesus was physically weak, the devil took the opportunity to tempt him by lying to him three times. The devil wanted to distract Jesus so he could change his mind about the fast and his commitment to God. I love Jesus's strategy in defeating the devil. In all three of the temptations, he used the Word to counter Satan's lies (Luke 4:4, 8, 12). *The Word is our weapon, which we have to use against Satan.*

Satan will always try to mess with our minds—to get us to think negatively and resist God. We, therefore, need to be conscious of what God's Word is saying about us. According to Jeremiah 29:11, God is interested in our future. He has a good plan for our lives. He definitely doesn't want disaster to befall us, but he desires that we prosper and succeed in all we do.

Do you believe God has equipped you with power, love, and a sound mind? Are you feeling discouraged, overwhelmed, or dissatisfied with your life? Then cry out to God. He has promised to shelter us with his loving arms in those moments of vulnerability. He is our loving heavenly Father, who looks out for our best interests. He has a great plan for our lives. Remember, he has blessed us with a sound mind—to think collectively and to make decisions that will please him.

Declaration

God, I know you haven't given me a spirit of fear, but you have given me a sound mind to make sensible decisions that will please and honor you. Therefore, I won't succumb to Satan's temptations; he wants to see me fall. But you will strengthen and enrich my life. I choose to look wholeheartedly to you because you have good things in store for me.

56

The Labels People Put on Us

Have you ever found yourself being so curious about seeing someone that you would do whatever it took to see that person? I think of Queen Elizabeth. When she visited our city a long time ago, crowds of people lined the streets just to get a glimpse of her. This incident reminds me of Zacchaeus in Luke 19. He was also determined to see Jesus, who was visiting his neighborhood that day.

I am sure Zacchaeus had heard many good reports about Jesus, so his curiosity to see him was even more heightened. However, he was too short, so he ran ahead of the crowd and climbed a sycamore-fig tree beside the road, hoping to see Jesus (Luke 19:2–4). Can you picture him up in the tree, waiting in anticipation for Jesus to pass by? You wonder—did he just want to get a good look at Jesus, or was his heart longing for something more?

Not only did Jesus know Zacchaeus was up in that tree, but he saw deep into his heart. He knew all the thoughts he was thinking, including his intentions, longings, and frustrations. Zacchaeus must have thought he was well hidden in that tree. I can imagine how shocked he was when Jesus looked up and called out to him, "Quick, come down! I must be a guest in your home today" (Luke 19:5). Can you imagine Zacchaeus's reaction? This was an opportunity he couldn't afford to miss. He was overjoyed, but the crowd was displeased. The people in that town had already labeled Zacchaeus as a "notorious sinner." As someone flawed. What kind of labels are people putting on you, or are you putting on yourself?

Thank goodness, Jesus's thoughts are so much different from ours.

Jesus plainly told Zacchaeus, "The Son of Man came to seek and save those who are lost" (Luke 19:10). This must have been a completely new doctrine for some of the religious groups. But, you see, Jesus isn't concerned about piousness and vanity, for he has come to save the lost—those who are broken, unloved, cast out, abandoned, and rejected by others. That's the reason he purposely sought out Zacchaeus. He was interested in his soul, his well-being. He saw his bleeding heart.

Zacchaeus hoped to get just one glimpse of Jesus, but Jesus had something much more in store for him. We may anticipate little droplets of blessings, but God always has something far beyond our imagination—something beautiful and worth waiting and living for. When life doesn't seem to offer us much, our portion seems scanty, or we find ourselves shutting down because we don't feel valued by others, what is our response? Or what is God saying to us?

Note: when Jesus told Zacchaeus he was going to his house, with great excitement he came down that tree and took Jesus to his house (v. 6). He didn't have second thoughts. I don't see him wondering whether Jesus would rebuke him for his dishonest lifestyle. Jesus's call to him was from a place of love and purity of heart. Jesus saw how much Zacchaeus was consumed with his crooked lifestyle. But he also saw there was a deep, burning desire in his heart to personally know this Jesus, whom he had been hearing about.

I'm sure Zacchaeus heard the grumblings of the townspeople. He saw the way they reacted. He must have felt their rejection. Their disapproval of his "notorious" lifestyle (Luke 19:7).

When Jesus comes on the scene, his purpose is always to bring transformation. In that house, as Jesus ministered to Zacchaeus, Zacchaeus's heart was drawn to Jesus's love, and God changed his heart. Zacchaeus couldn't refrain from making this beautiful commitment: "I will give half [of] my wealth to the poor, Lord, and if I have cheated people on their taxes, I will give them back four times as much!" (Luke 19:8). I'm sure if the critics were in that room, it would have blown their minds. But not Jesus. When he comes in, we do not hold onto past sins. *We do the great exploits we are supposed to do* (Daniel 11:32).

Yes, new commitments will take place. Our minds will open to God and his ways. His purpose for our lives will matter more than anything else.

It is no wonder Jesus told Zacchaeus, "Salvation has come to this home today" (Luke 19:9). Indeed, when we commit our lives to God, we will experience his delivering power. We will experience joy.

Does anything from the past hold you back from being all God wants you to be? Start saying, "I am not functioning in what held me back in the past anymore." If people's criticism and their reaction to your past lifestyle made you lack courage, now declare, "When Jesus sees me, he sees my potential, not my setbacks and flaws." At this moment, Jesus wants you to know he is *not* angry with you; his kindness won't depart from you. His covenant of peace won't be removed from you (Isaiah 54:9–10). Like Zacchaeus Jesus has come to put a new label on your life. Tell yourself the following.

Declaration

God has given me a new start.

"[I am] God's masterpiece. He has created [me] anew in Christ Jesus, so [I] can do the good things he planned for [me] long ago" (Ephesians 2:10). Salvation has come to my house, so now I will walk in God's ways. The Lord is now my Savior and Redeemer. He has set me free from past sins. Through Christ, I have a new life. He has a beautiful plan for my life.

57

What a Friend We Have in Jesus

What a friend we have in Jesus,
All our sins and griefs to bear!
What a privilege to carry,
Everything to God in prayer!
—Joseph Medlicott Scriven (1819–1886)

Aren't there times when you feel like you need to talk to someone who is loyal and genuine? Someone who will listen to you and not judge you? The song says it's a privilege to carry all our sins and griefs to Jesus, our true friend. He is the one to whom we can unload our burdened hearts. It's a time when you talk to God in prayer, especially when your emotions are going wild and you don't even understand yourself. Other times, the people around you aren't applauding you but rejecting or criticizing you. These are the moments when you can share with Jesus any and everything on your mind. In fact, this is the best and perfect time to go to God. According to Psalm 33:15, God made our hearts, so he understands us through and through: every fiber in our being, every pain we feel, including our motives, the whole situation from beginning to end—and even when we mess up.

What does it really mean to have God as our Friend?

Friendship demands trust, loyalty, and commitment. Do you have such a friend who fits these qualities? If the answer is no, that's okay. Jesus/God is such a friend. We are always on God's mind. Because he has our best interest at heart, he will not let us down or forget about us. In fact, he firmly tells us, "Can a mother forget the baby at her breast and have no compassion on the child she has borne? Though she may forget, I will not forget you!" (Isaiah 49:15 NIV). This is the depth of God's love for us; it is even stronger than a mother's love. God knows us by name, and he cares about each detail of our lives.

God's love is unfailing and unchangeable. In moments when we need answers or there seem to be roadblocks, like the writer of Psalm 32, let's tell God, "You are my hiding place; you will protect me from trouble. You surround me with songs of deliverance" (v. 7 NIV). When we feel unsettled or disturbed about circumstances, we need to lean on someone who will help and comfort us. That's when God will come to our rescue. As we hide in him, not only will he protect us, but he also promises to surround us with songs of victory. This means God will make a way and turn our trouble and pain into a song. Instead of worrying, we will be singing.

God is indeed a true friend. Finding some time to talk with him will make all the difference to our well-being. In his presence, we will find a safe hiding place, where he will encourage and strengthen us. He won't allow the enemy or circumstances to destroy or overwhelm us. He will come to our rescue and hide us under his wings of love.

In times of discouragement or trouble, do you call on the name of the Lord? Running to God in prayer is the greatest privilege we can ever have. There, you will find out God is your strong fortress; he will keep you safe, hopeful, and confident. If for some reason your faith is wavering and you are doubtful about what is happening around you, be assured that God is with you throughout the entire process. You aren't struggling in the dark all alone. His everlasting arms will comfort and guide you until you see the victory. Now, begin to praise God for his steadfast love.

Praise Moment

Lord, you are my strength, fortress, and refuge. When I am in distress or feeling lonely and vulnerable, I will come to you. I know you will keep me safe, peaceful, and strong. Lord, thank you for being my friend at all times. In every season and in every circumstance, I know I can always count on you to be there for me. You will never fail me.

God's Beautiful Grace Encounters Hearts

> My grace is sufficient for you, for my strength is made
> perfect in [those areas of weakness in your life].
> —2 Corinthians 12:9 (NKJV)

God freely gives us his grace because of his great love and compassion for mankind. God's grace is fierce; it sweeps through territories, rooms, and all kinds of environments; and it encounters hearts, as illustrated in the story of the prodigal son in Luke 15. Whatever got into his mind, one day the prodigal son "said to his father, 'Father, give me the portion of goods that falls to me'" (Luke 15:12 NKJV). Impulsively he set off for a distant country, where he became so destitute that he even had to eat the pods the pigs were eating. In other words, he was in a total mess, but his condition didn't miss God's eyes. Grace can reach us, even in a pigsty!

Suddenly, the prodigal son realized he was penniless, hungry, and in rags. Not only had he lost his way because of the irrational choices he had made, but he had ruined his relationship with his father. In the pigsty, aware of his impoverished condition, he decided to return home. That's how the grace of God works. It will encounter us and give us the strength and courage to do something positive about our situation. I'm glad the prodigal son "came to himself" (Luke 15:17 NKJV). This is where the turning point begins. When the grace of God encounters us, we come to terms with ourselves. We look deeply inside; *we don't stay stuck in the mess* or destructive habits we might find ourselves in. We turn to God for help. We even become desperate for God to intervene in our lives.

When the prodigal son returned home, his father welcomed him, showing love and compassion to him. The father was so overcome with joy that he "said to his servants, 'Bring out *the best robe* and put it on him, and put a ring on his hand and sandals on his feet'" (Luke 15:20–22 NKJV, emphasis added). Giving his son the best robe, sandals, and a ring is a representation of the *good things* our heavenly Father has in store for us. God has the best in store for us. He will forgive us for all our sins and remember them no more. Like the prodigal son, let's throw off those rags—the old paths that didn't please God—and return to him. Because of God's unfailing love for us, he will give us another chance to serve him and will clothe us with his righteousness. This means we can now stand righteous before God.

God's purpose is always to draw people to himself. Even when we stray from God's path, he will relentlessly go after us. Moreover, he will rebuild us, so that once more we will be filled with peace and joy, and will have a reason to live. Since only God can change our hearts and life course, his call is compelling. He knows all the other pleasures in life are just temporary; they aren't fulfilling.

Despite all his imperfections, rebellion, and desire to do his own thing, the prodigal son still experienced the grace of God. It doesn't matter where we find ourselves or how deep we have fallen; God's steadfast love doesn't change.

Without a doubt, the pigsty was filthy and smelly. To

the human eyes, it definitely isn't a place we will look to for possibilities or opportunities. It may even seem as out of bounds for anything good to come out of that mess. Thank goodness God's ways are far higher than our imagination. That pigsty was the very place God chose to demonstrate his power. Yes, God's grace is sufficient for all kinds of messy situations. No exception. When grace shows up, it perfects us. And those weak areas become strong (2 Corinthians 12:9).

Like the prodigal son, do you feel the strong call of God's Spirit drawing you back to him? Can you picture what happened to the prodigal son when he went home and his father received him unreservedly? I am sure it was a moment when his mourning turned into joy, and he made a firm decision to follow God's path. Even now, "as we confess our sins, [God] is faithful and just to forgive us our sins and to cleanse us from all unrighteousness" (1 John 1:9 (ESV). Let's take some time to give God praise for his grace, which he has freely given to us.

Prayer

God, thank you for your grace, which reached out to me when I didn't deserve it. I surrender my entire life to you again. Thank you for forgiving me for every sin I have ever committed. Because of your grace, I now stand righteous in your eyes. Amen.

We Are More Than Conquerors

There is another power within [us] that is at
war with [our] mind. This power makes [us] a
slave to the sin that is still within [us].
—Romans 7:23

Based on the above verse, there is a war going on within us between the Holy Spirit and our old, sinful nature. For that reason, we must stay alert and watch out for the devil, who is always on the lookout to tempt us so we can fall into sin. Even worse, he will try to enslave us in sin. The devil is our greatest enemy.

A picture of the enemy's gates in my mind gave me a clearer understanding of how evil and cunning Satan really is. I imagined those huge iron gates with the enemy inside, just waiting for me to enter so he could tear me up into pieces. That picture is a representation of how Satan operates. His number-one purpose is to get God's people to enter the "gates of sin." For that reason, he sets up strategies for God's people to get into activities that don't please our heavenly Father.

Satan, the greatest schemer of all time, uses temptations to get people to disobey God. That's what happened in the garden of Eden. In Genesis 3:1–3, we see that Eve was having a conversation with the serpent (Satan). Before, she wasn't even thinking about eating the forbidden fruit. Previously, God had warned her and Adam that if they ate of that fruit, they would die, so they were keenly obeying God's command until the serpent showed up.

The devil lied to Eve, telling her, "You will not certainly die, for God knows that when you eat from it your eyes will be opened, and you will be like God, knowing good and evil" (Genesis 3:4–5 NIV). Isn't this exactly how the devil works? He *puts ideas in our minds* so we can sin. Soon afterward, Eve started to think about what the serpent had told her. Instead of saying no to those wrong thoughts, her mind started to think that maybe the serpent was right, so she yielded to the temptation.

Not very long after Eve "saw that the fruit of the tree was good for food and pleasing to the eye, and also desirable for gaining wisdom, she took some and ate it. She also gave some to her husband, who was with her, and he ate it" (Genesis 3:6 NIV). Isn't this a clear illustration of how Satan tries to entice us?

Satan crafts temptations to look so beautiful and appealing that we fall right into sin. Note: *the devil will never tell us the aftermath of falling into temptation.* He knows perfectly well how we will feel when we obey Satan rather than our heavenly Father, so he conceals the consequences. Eve and Adam never suspected that eating the forbidden fruit would make them feel so horrible. That's the reason they hid from God (Genesis 3:8).

If perchance you have fallen into sin, God has already provided a way for you. You don't need to continue being in sin.

Some pointers to deal with sin:

- "Come now, and let us reason together. Though your sins are like scarlet, they shall be as white as snow. Though they are red like crimson, they shall be as wool" (Isaiah 1:18 NKJV).
  God is actually reaffirming that he will wash away and cleanse us from all our past sins.
- "Resist [the devil], [and stay] steadfast in the faith" (1 Peter 5:8–9 NKJV).
  This means we have to choose to resist the devil and stay committed to Jesus.
  "God is working in you, giving you the desire and the power to do what pleases him" (Philippians 2:13).
  Remember, those wrong desires don't have to overtake us to the point that we obey them. Instead, let's set our minds on the things of the Spirit, who gives us the desire and power to do what pleases him. Yes, God will empower us with inner strength through the Holy Spirit.
- "We are more than conquerors through Him who loved us" (Romans 8:37 NKJV).
  Because of the Holy Spirit's beautiful work in our lives, we are *more than conquerors* over temptations.

Even as we decide to stand strong and refuse to enter the gates of the enemy, be assured that God will send his angels to strengthen us and deliver us from every temptation that would ever come our way.

Do you know that Satan is using all kinds of strategies to get us to listen to him? Notice, Satan lied to Eve so she could desire the fruit. Isn't this how temptation works? *The devil will find a way to get us to desire it.* He makes sure it's the perfect strategy so we stay in that particular place where the temptation is. He knows that if we can stay there long enough, we won't be able to resist it; then we will fall into sin. What a crafty setup by Satan. Even now tell God about the wrong desires in our hearts.

Prayer

Lord, I will be watchful because the devil is purposely going after my mind to fill it with wrong thoughts and desires. Thank you for making a way for me to overcome sin. I now possess supernatural power to fight temptations because of the Holy Spirit, who is living inside me.

60

God's Mercy Gives Us a Fresh Start

Through the Lord's mercies we are not consumed,
Because His compassions fail not. They are new every
morning; Great is Your faithfulness. "The Lord is my
portion," says my soul, "Therefore I hope in Him!"
—Lamentations. 3:22–26 (NKJV)

God's mercies begin afresh each morning. Isn't it amazing
that God will actually look beyond all our wrongdoings,
past mistakes, and faults and choose to give us a fresh start?
Spending time with God in the morning is a great way to start
the day. Over and over again, I would get up in the morning
and feel that I'd wasted my time the day before or simply didn't
do what the Holy Spirit had urged me to do. But when morning
hits, I would literally feel the faithful love of God pouring into
my life one more time. That's because of God's character—he
is merciful and kind, and his love is genuine.

The beauty about God is that he doesn't reject us, condemn
us, or judge us if we've messed up or made a huge mistake.
Actually, God wants to woo us back into his love like a lover
would pursue the one he loves. That's God showing us his
mercy. He's a loving Father, who doesn't drag our past failures
and sins into the present and future. Isn't this mind blowing?

We don't need to be burdened with our past weaknesses, flaws, and mistakes anymore. But we do need to do something about them. We need to bring them to the cross and leave them there. As we quietly wait in his presence, let us make this decision to seek and run after him with all our hearts. Because of God's faithful love and mercy, he will forgive us of all our sins and give us a fresh start.

God is indeed merciful. Mercy speaks of the forgiving nature of God. He's a God of second chances, who doesn't hold our sins against us. If we made mistakes or stumbled in the past, God will forgive us. That's because God is kindhearted. In his eyes, the sins we committed in the past never happened. That's how much God loves us. His love for us is true; he will look beyond all our faults and lead us in the right way.

God is always looking down on earth. Many times he sees the struggles people are going through because they can't forgive themselves for past mistakes or sins. Have you forgiven yourself for the past? If so, then God has given you a fresh start.

According to Romans 8:1–2, "there is no condemnation for those who belong to Christ Jesus. And because you belong to him, the power of the life-giving Spirit has freed you from the power of sin." This means God won't condemn us for past mistakes; he has forgiven us. Therefore, we shouldn't be carrying guilt or feel unworthy or ashamed. We actually belong to God; he loves us unconditionally. As we surrender to him, God's strong hand will hold us securely. He will not let us fall to the wiles of Satan or the evil influence of the world. Now we belong to God, and the Spirit has freed us from the power of sin (Romans 8:2).

Do you believe God knows and cares about all the past failures and blunders you have made in the past? Have you been beating yourself up? Or not forgiving yourself? The writer of Lamentations reminds us that God's mercies are new every morning. This means it doesn't matter how far you have strayed from God or how many wrongs you have done, *God's mercy is still available to you!* As you decide to serve him, this is the perfect time for you to thank God for being merciful and kind to you.

Declaration

Because of your faithful love and tender mercies, I now abandon my past sins and wrongdoings. I choose a new path for my life, where I will now serve and obey you with all my heart.

Good Choices

Throughout the day, we consciously or unconsciously make choices about tasks, assignments, commitments, and the way we should behave. How we respond to these decisions can either make us or break us. In some cases, we might end up not doing the right thing, so we need to deal with the repercussions that follow. Other times, we need to deal with the heavy burden of unforgiveness, addiction, or various temptations we might fall into. Although these are challenging decisions, the chapters in "Good Choices" will make you realize you can run into the arms of a heavenly Father and bring all your issues to him. This could be the defining moment you have long been waiting for—the moment when you encounter God's love and start a brand-new journey. With God himself! His continuous work in our hearts sets the tone for us to make right, wholesome decisions. As new faith and courage fill our hearts, we will see that God honors and rewards us for the godly choices we make.

61

Running, Yet God's Love Follows

[God] does not punish us for all our sins; he does
not deal harshly with us, as we deserve.
—Psalm 103:10.

How many times have you made mistakes you regret? Our very
words and actions can cause us to get into trouble. In the book
of Genesis, we see one mistake after another. First, instead of
Sarai trusting God to give her a child, she "took her Egyptian
slave Hagar and gave her to her husband to be his wife. He
slept with Hagar, and she conceived. When she knew she was
pregnant, she began to despise her mistress ... [As a result],
Sarai mistreated Hagar; so she fled from her" (Genesis 16:3–6
NIV). Neither of these women acted right, but Hagar was the
one who ran away.

Mistakes are inevitable, yet so many times, we can get so
caught up with them and get so discouraged that we can even
lose sight of God. For some people, the mistake seems too big in
their eyes. But when we make a mistake, what is God thinking
about us? Does he punish us harshly or write us off?

Notice, when Hagar made a mistake, she ran away from her
mistress, but God still chased after her—not to condemn her
but to encourage her. Amid her pregnancy, God sent his angel,

who told her to name the child Ishmael, which means "the Lord has heard of your misery" (Genesis 16:11 NIV). Wow, God sees when we are struggling. He pays close attention to our misery and frustration. Hagar was so grateful for encountering the angel that she exclaimed, "You are the God who sees me, I have now seen the One who sees me" (Genesis 16:13 NIV).

Hagar then understood that although she had messed up, God still cared about her well-being. She was all alone in the wilderness. God had seen how broken she was and had come to her rescue. Indeed, *the Lord is a God of seeing*! God knew what Hagar was thinking and how abandoned and distraught she must have felt because of her wrongdoing. Yes, we go through pain when we make mistakes. But this is the very moment when God wants to draw near to us and strengthen and help us.

When we blunder or make wrong decisions, God doesn't give up on us. *His plan is never to destroy us* but to bring us back to him. As a matter of fact, he sees far beyond our imagination and perception. In fact, God has good plans for our lives. He deeply cares about our future. He doesn't want our lives to be ruined by bad decision-making or a purposeless lifestyle, but he wants to give us a future filled with hope and good opportunities.

When the angel found Hagar near a spring of water in the desert, he said to her, "Go back to your mistress and submit to her" (Genesis 16:7, 9 NIV). Whenever we make a mistake, being submissive to authority is an important step to take. In this case, Hagar needed to submit to Sarai. When we, as individuals, make a mistake, we first need to come humbly before God and submit to him. God is compassionate; he will not accuse us or stay angry with us. In fact, he will continue to show us his unfailing love so we can repent, fix our mistake, and continue to serve him.

Have you made a mistake that is holding you back? Or causing you much stress? Note: despite Hagar's mistake, the angel reminded her about God's future purposes for her life and her son's. Through her son, many generations would be born, whom he would multiply exceedingly (Genesis 16:10 NKJV). Whenever we are reminded of God's purpose for our lives, God will always give us hope for the future. If a past mistake is troubling you, why not confess it and talk to the Lord about it? Remember, God doesn't stay angry with us or punish us for our sins. He shows us mercy (Psalm 103:9–11 NKJV). As you commit your life to God, share the following with him.

Commitment

Lord, thank you that you don't deal harshly with us as we deserve. However, I know you want me to turn from my wrong ways, so I surrender my entire life to you. Now I have a *brand-new purpose* for my life. I'm on a fresh journey to fulfill all you would want me to do. Amen.

62

A Brand-New Journey

Take delight in the Lord, and he will give you the
desires of your heart. Commit your way to the
LORD; trust in him and he will do this: He will make
your righteous reward shine like the dawn.
—Psalm 37:4–6 (NIV)

Everyone at some point has to look back and re-evaluate his or her life. We may even realize it's time for a change. It's time for a brand-new lifestyle—a new purpose, a fresh journey. You know God has created you on this earth for a specific purpose, which you are determined to pursue.

You have been carrying this goal, dream, or desire for a long time. You are longing to see it fulfilled. It starts with a decision, a new mindset. It starts with a new attitude of being optimistic, hopeful, and confident. Now your new aspiration is to put all your energies into going after that dream God has so markedly put in your heart. You know achieving that dream will bring you the fulfillment, peace, and joy you desire.

In the past, that dream just sat there—dormant, hidden, and unexpressed.

As you reflect on the past, your goal is to get rid of all negativity: failures, disappointments, mistakes, frustrations, heartaches—whatever had ruffled your feathers or kept you from fulfilling God's call on your life. This means we need to be determined and dedicated to whatever God is telling us to do. Like the apostle Paul, we need to declare, "One thing I do, forgetting those things which are behind and reaching forward to those things which are ahead, *I press toward the goal* for the prize of the upward call of God in Christ Jesus" (Philippians 3:13–14 NKJV, emphasis added).

Some things from the past you want to bring before the Lord, with the intention of leaving them behind.

Voices within
Command, initiate
Choices that captivate
Together they shook my faith.
Together they labeled me failure
Those labels kept me from my knees.
Sanity, Worth, Victory: I could not seize
Then bias, distortion, untruth—all chimed in:
Their words, "How hard you try, you still can't win."
Stabbed me to the core. No fight was left in me for sure;
Just guilt, condemnation, shame. How they assaulted me!
My cry broke out, "Why, did you make me so weak, so blind?"
"Oh," my soul cried. "Those I recall, have curbed my every shine!"
Yes, the weight of sin got wider, *bigger.* It truly stained my very mind!

Based on the illustration above, bigger is definitely *not* better. Clearly, this diagram depicts the deception that happens in our minds. It's one of Satan's strategies to make mistakes and flaws *look so big* that they overwhelm and defeat us. Although we might have committed those mistakes or sins in the past, Satan makes sure he plagues our minds as if they are in the present.

Yes, the weight of sin will feel heavier and *bigger* to the point that it can stain our minds. This happens because Satan reminds us of the wrongdoings of the past so we can become burdened with feelings of rejection, condemnation, guilt, hurt, and shame. These emotions will all weigh us down and prevent us from accepting God's love for us. You may even feel God doesn't love you anymore, which would weaken your faith in him and bring doubt and fear as to whether God would accept you or not.

Currently, what is your life like? Is the past hindering you from moving forward? Because of God's abundant love for mankind, he doesn't count our sins and shortcomings against us. God wants to free us from every kind of sin. These vices just condemn us and cloud our minds from accepting God's beautiful plan for our lives. Through Jeremiah 29:11 (AMP), God says to us. "I know the plans and thoughts that I have for you, plans for peace and well-being and not for disaster, to give you a future and a hope." Start believing that God has good things in store for you.

Commitment

Lord, I commit my life to you afresh. My faith is stirred again to believe you have a *great plan for my life*. I will follow your path; I want you to take the lead in my life. Amen.

63

The Bondage of Addiction

I am allowed to do anything—but not everything is good for you. And even though I am allowed to do anything, I must not become a slave to anything.
—1 Corinthians 6:12

I remember standing in my kitchen and deciding what to eat for breakfast. On the counter were many delicious treats I really loved to indulge in. That morning I felt the Lord saying to me, "Don't touch those." You see, many years ago, I had been a big-time binger. I had gone through many emotional problems; actually, it was a serious depression, during which, eating had become my outlet. Over time, not only had I gained a tremendous amount of weight, but I had developed an eating disorder that greatly affected almost every phase of my life.

Even now as I am writing this, I know many people have had different kinds of disorders, addictions, or problems they are dealing with that seem uncontrollable. Not being able to break certain habits isn't something to be ashamed of. It's just that you have gotten into a lifestyle that is preventing you from being free. Maybe without even realizing it, you have become addicted. Think for a moment. What is an addiction? Is it that thing you hate so much and so badly want to stop doing? But you still find yourself doing it?

Thank goodness, you can come to a place where you admit that you do have a difficult time trying to free yourself from that addiction. Maybe you are asking, "Where do I go from here?" This is the exact place where God wants to come right in. It's a time for decision-making when you need to choose to deal with those seemingly uncontrollable desires connected to that addiction. First, you need to come to the realization that those desires don't need to control you. Tell yourself, *"Those desires are no longer my master*; I want to be free! I will be free! God has designed me to be free!"*

What course of action are you planning to take to free yourself from this addiction? Some people acknowledge the problem and choose to go to a professional for counseling sessions to get further help. Others know their healing lies in their willingness to come to the cross, where they will receive his mercy and grace to help in times when they need him (Hebrews 4:16 NKJV). The cross is the place where we choose to be honest and transparent before God. It's the place where we meet a loving God who "understands our weaknesses, for he faced all of the same testings as we do, yet he did not sin" (Hebrews 4:15).

How does it make you feel that Jesus identifies with your weakness to the point that he wants to deliver you? This is what happened to the woman caught in the act of adultery in John 8.

One morning the scribes and Pharisees brought this woman to Jesus. They believed she should be stoned for her sinful act (John 8:2–5). The people's purpose for bringing her to Jesus was to shame her and trap Jesus. But Jesus responded to them by saying, "He who is without sin among you, let him throw a stone at her first" (John 8:7 NKJV). Note: Jesus knew their evil thoughts. But he had another thought; he wanted to free this woman from her sinful path of life. That's *Jesus identifying with her weakness and showing her grace.* Afterward, he told her he didn't condemn her for what she had done, but she shouldn't stay in the practice of sin (John 8:10–11). In other words, Jesus was actually letting her know the grace of God was sufficient to deliver her from this sin. Where sin or addiction is dominant, grace is far greater.

Do you believe Jesus identifies with your weakness or addiction? As you come to the cross, *God's grace will empower you to overcome sin.* I myself had to deal with this eating disorder. Although I wasn't set free right away, as I kept going to the cross, little by little, God delivered me. As you embrace God's love, let him do his work of cleansing and delivering you, and God will indeed set you free. Now it's time to set your heart on God, not to go back to the pleasure of sin. Declare the following:

Declaration

Lord, I come to the cross, giving myself completely to you. "Because of that cross, my interest in this world has been crucified, and the world's interest in me has also died" (Galatians 6:14).

64

God Honors Godly Choices

Are there obstacles in your life preventing you from making good, godly choices? Or are they keeping you from staying true to God? In the book of Daniel, Daniel and his three friends—Hananiah, Mishael, and Azariah (known as Shadrach, Meshach, and Abednego)—from the tribe of Judah were exiled in Babylon. There these young men faced many challenges.

Daniel 1 recounts the story of Daniel. King Nebuchadnezzar assigned Daniel and his three friends a specific diet comprising a daily amount of food and wine. Also, they had to go through training for three years (Daniel 1:5). However, Daniel decided that he wouldn't *defile himself* with the king's delicacies. He viewed the food and wine of the king as unacceptable to partake of. For that reason, with consent from the attendant, he was given a diet of vegetables and water.

Daniel's stance rests in the fact that he wanted to adhere to what was best for his health and what was pleasing in God's eyes. Because Daniel made an important choice, "Daniel and his three friends looked healthier and better nourished than all of the young men who ate the royal food" (Daniel 1:15 NIV). When we make good choices, not only are they rewarding, but God will be pleased with us.

Later, as seen in Daniel 3, Shadrach, Meshach, and Abednego were faced with another dilemma; this one was even life threatening. Again, they made a godly choice. They refused to bow down to the golden statue King Nebuchadnezzar had demanded everyone should bow down to (Daniel 3:12). Placed in such a position, what would have been your response? Would you have bowed to the statue like everyone else, or would you have obeyed the Lord?

Shadrach, Meshach, and Abednego's decision of not bowing down to the statue made the king very furious (Daniel 3:19). But he still gave them one more chance. But these guys didn't look at it as an opportunity to save themselves from death; their hearts were set on worshipping their God, the only true God they knew. Refusing to worship the statue, they boldly told the king, "We want to make it clear to you, Your Majesty, that we will never serve your gods or worship the gold statue you have set up" (Daniel 3:18). What a tenacious stand! As a result, these boys were cast into the fire. I'm so thrilled to find out that their God didn't leave them in the fire; he delivered them in an amazing way.

Right in that blazing fire, Nebuchadnezzar observed that these men were walking around the fire, unharmed. Then the king had a huge surprise, and he couldn't refrain himself from exclaiming, "Look! I see four men loose, walking in the midst of the fire; and they are not hurt, and the form of the fourth is like the Son of God" (Daniel 3:25 NKJV). God himself was in the fire with these young men. Thank goodness when we are in the fire, God is still faithful.

Nebuchadnezzar was amazed to see God's miraculous power. He knew these young men were untouched by the fire because God had sent his angels to protect them. What a miracle they all experienced! These young men's courage and loyalty to their God made the king realize their God was the true God. He is a Rescuer and Deliverer in times of trouble. These men trusted in their God, and he didn't disappoint them.

Are you in a situation where you're not sure how it will end? When the three guys were placed in such a life-threatening situation, they didn't know how it would turn out. But they dared to put their trust in God. Even Nebuchadnezzar afterward exclaimed, "They defied the king's command and were willing to die rather than serve or worship any god except their own God" (Daniel 3:28). Like these three young men, are you willing to stand up for your faith? These boys stood the test, and as a result, an angelic presence manifested. As you think over your life, reflect on God's greatness and delivering power, and make a fresh commitment to God.

Prayer

Let a holy tenacity rise in our hearts, O Lord. We make this choice to serve you, to forsake anything that would come between our God and our souls. We choose *only* what would please you, Lord. Your will matters more than anything else. Amen.

65

Shake Off Temptations

Let no one say when he is tempted, "I am
tempted by God"; for God cannot be tempted by
evil, nor does He Himself tempt anyone.
—James 1:13 (NKJV)

The devil has tempted all of us at one point or another in our lives. Even Jesus faced temptations. One important fact about temptation is that when a person is tempted, he or she cannot say he or she is tempted by God, because God doesn't tempt anyone. A temptation itself isn't a sin. However, when we are faced with a temptation and yield to it, we sin.

According to James 1:14–15, "Temptation comes from our own desires, which entice us and drag us away from doing what God wants us to do. These desires give birth to sinful actions. And when sin is allowed to grow, it gives birth to death." Clearly, when we sin, we are the ones responsible for our actions; actually, we are drawn into sin by our own selfish and lustful desires. For example, we might see something or someone who attracts us, and then we desire to have that person or thing. Although nothing is wrong with desiring something or someone, if it's a wrong desire, then we need to stay far away from that person or thing.

Where do wrong desires originate from? Jeremiah 17:9 (NKJV) tells us that "The heart is deceitful above all things, And desperately wicked; who can know it?" Those wrong desires start from deep within, because of that old sinful nature we are all born into. If we find ourselves battling wrong desires, more than likely we might start to think of ways to fulfill that desire, so the desire becomes stronger and stronger. Then that desire waits for a chance to act out what is in the mind, and when the opportunity arises, that person will find out that he or she doesn't have the power to resist the temptation.

James is therefore warning us that the wrong thoughts and desires we conceive can give birth to sin, which will produce spiritual death. From inception, it is never God's intention for his children to fall into sin. Thankfully, God is faithful, and he will not allow us to be tempted to the point that we can't handle or bear it, but when we are tempted he promises to "show [us] a way out so that [we] can endure" and overcome it (1 Corinthians 10:13).

How does God make a way for us to escape sin? Here are a few pointers to help us resist temptation:

- If you find yourself in the place where the temptation exists, don't sit around in that area and let the temptation stare at you (or you at it). Walk away, saying, "I will let the Holy Spirit guide my life. Then I won't be doing what my sinful nature craves" (Galatians 5:16).

In a nutshell, the apostle Paul cautioned us about how easily we can fall into sin because of our sinful natures. He wants us to be conscious about the paths we take, the places we go, the thoughts we think, and the activities we are involved in.

- What's even more important is that we need to depend on the Holy Spirit, because the "Holy Spirit helps us in our weakness" (Romans 8:26).

  Because the Father understands the depths of our hearts, he knows exactly when we are feeling vulnerable. The Holy Spirit is right there to work with us until we come to the place where we are in harmony with God's will.

- Let's declare who we are in Christ because of the Holy Spirit living inside us. "I am strong in the Lord and in the power of His might!" (Ephesians 6:10 NKJV).

  God has provided a much better way for us, As we depend on the Holy Spirit, we will be equipped with his strength to live a victorious Christian life.

- Be aware of Satan's schemes. When he tries to tempt you, tell him, "I will submit myself to God. I will resist the devil, and in this way I will not give in to the desires of the flesh" (James 4:7 NKJV).

  We, therefore, need to make the choice—to be committed to our faith in Jesus. We will resist the devil and draw near to God.

According to Romans 8:11 (ESV), the Holy Spirit dwells in us; it is the same Spirit who raised Jesus from the dead. This means we have his resurrection power in us. The Holy Spirit in us will now cause the supernatural to become active in our lives. Therefore, now we are no more living this Christian life in our own strength and ability. A greater power—the Holy Spirit—is now at work in our lives.

Do you believe the Lord will help you in that area of weakness? This is a moment for us to look deeply into our lives. First, examine the kind of activities you are involved in. Next, ask yourself whether they are building your life. If they are not, then you need to decide to listen carefully to what God is saying to you. A great place to start is by reading Psalm 119. Also, Proverbs is another good book to read. Praying, reading the Word, speaking to faith-believing Christians, being obedient, and making good, godly decisions will provide you with strength, courage, and power to overcome every temptation that will ever cross your path. Even now, declare the following:

Declaration

God, I completely surrender my life to you. From this day onward, I choose to please you in all my ways. I won't let myself think of ways to indulge my evil desires. This means I will now rely on the Holy Spirit, who will help me to overcome any kind of sin. No temptation is too strong for me not to break or overcome. Through the Holy Spirit, I will now live a victorious life.

66

Praise Changes Us

As we walk through the streets or observe people on the buses and trains, we might notice that everywhere we go, people are complaining and grumbling about something or someone. Or they are simply seeing the negative side instead of the positive side of any given situation.

However, as we look at Psalm 100:1–5, we see an altogether different picture. The psalmist is drawing our attention to thanksgiving and praise, the very gateway to the presence of God, when our entire being surrenders to the sovereignty of God. This is when our bad attitudes and perspectives about our situation change, and our lips are filled with praise and adoration instead of negativity.

Let's join the psalmist as he declares,

- "Shout for joy to the Lord, all the earth. Worship the Lord with gladness" (Psalm 100:1 NIV).
- God loves when we, his children, decide to open our hearts to him and worship him. I believe that in worship the Holy Spirit does his most beautiful work in our hearts and fills us with singing and gladness instead of mourning and heaviness.
- "Come before him with joyful songs" (v. 2 NIV).

- "Come" speaks of humbly surrendering our wills to God. It's a time to let go of all the burdens and anxieties we are carrying. Instead, we choose to sing and praise God, believing he will take care of all that's on our minds.
- "Know that the Lord is God" (v. 3 NIV).

This means I come to an understanding that Jehovah God is *personally my God*, who loves me with an everlasting love. I am confident he is all powerful—no one is above him. Every other power has to bow before him.

- "It is [God] who made us, and we are his; we are his people, the sheep of his pasture" (v. 3 NIV).

This verse assures us that we belong to God, no matter what thing or person has a claim on us. We therefore should choose to worship him with all our hearts, knowing that like a good shepherd, he will lead us in paths of righteousness, and in the pathway that leads to peace and joy.

- "Enter his gates with thanksgiving and his courts with praise; give thanks to him and praise his name" (v. 4 NIV).

Thanksgiving and praise—the very gateway to God's presence. As we think about the many good things, such as our accomplishments, the jobs God has provided, and all that God has done for us, how can we not praise and worship him? God is pleased when we honor him. In the first place, he is the one who has provided all the good things and privileges we possess.

"For the Lord is good and his love endures forever" (v. 5 NIV).

This verse sums up God's true character: he is good, and his love is unfailing, which gives us hope amid adverse and hopeless situations. Instead of living in fear and anxiety, we can trust in God's goodness, knowing he will not fail or forsake us. The fact that God has our backs gives us an even better reason to worship and praise him.

- "His faithfulness continues through all generations" (v. 5 NIV).

God is interested in future generations. He wants each generation to experience all the good things he has in store for them. His intention is always for us to have *the best life ever*—filled with victories, joy, peace, and righteousness.

Is there an obstacle in your path preventing you from praising God? As we go through life, we sometimes have to deal with all kinds of pressure, frustration, and problems, but taking some time off to praise him will change our perspective about our situation and ultimately those bad feelings. The language of Psalm 100 is full of praise and adoration to God, and it reminds us of God's faithfulness and unfailing love. As you read this psalm, God will restore your strength, vitality, and joy. Even now, take a moment to praise God.

Praise Moment

Lord, I am thankful that I belong to you. You are a good Shepherd, who will lead me on peaceful and righteous paths. I praise you for the many good things you have provided for me and my family.

Let Intercession Fire Burn

Have you ever felt intercession pouring into your life because of a hostile environment you found yourself in? This is what happened to Hannah. First Samuel 1 recounts the story of the conflict between Hannah and Peninnah, the two wives of Elkanah. While Peninnah had children, Hannah had none. Because Hannah was barren, Peninnah made a point of letting her become conscious of her condition. "So it was, year by year, when she went up to the house of the Lord, that she provoked her; therefore she wept and did not eat" (1 Samuel 1:7 NKJV).

Can you imagine how Hannah must have felt deep inside? Being in such an uncomfortable environment is always nerve racking. But something about a hostile environment can drive you. It drove Hannah to her knees. I can picture Hannah telling God about all the insults and demeaning words she had heard, but at the same time, she didn't forget to ask God to forgive Peninnah.

In intercessory prayer, letting go of negativity or anything that will stop God from moving is important. Mark 11:25 says, "When you are praying, first forgive anyone you are holding a grudge against, so that your Father in heaven will forgive your sins, too." I am sure Hannah knew that for her to receive answers to her prayers, she had to let go of others' wrongdoings. She couldn't hold on to a grudge. I can picture Hannah emptying her soul of everything that didn't line up with forgiveness and God's will.

Hannah was broken before God. Whether she was pacing the floor, bowing down, or prostrating herself on the floor, to the priest she appeared as if she had been drinking (1 Samuel 1:13 NKJV). But Hannah was in deep intercession. Her soul was connecting to a mighty God. A faithful God. A prayer-answering God.

In that moment of great anguish and sorrow, as intercession fire started to burn deep in her heart, Hannah's womb was opened. At such a pivotal moment, God revealed to the priest that he would grant her request. The Lord didn't forget Hannah's prayers, because "it came to pass in the process of time that Hannah conceived and bore a son, and called his name Samuel, saying, 'Because I have asked for him from the Lord'" (1 Samuel 1:20 NKJV). Yes, Hannah went through much pain and discomfort, but I'm sure when she held her son in her arms, she became more aware of God's goodness and faithfulness. She knew her God didn't fail or forsake her; in a desperate time, he answered her cry.

Dealing with her own barrenness and Peninnah's mockery must have made Hannah hold on to God even more. I believe Hannah learned to lean on God, her Rock. When you have no one else to lean on or to pour your heart out to, God has promised to always be there for us. During dark circumstances, let's cry out to God, knowing he will not fail us. In fact, take shelter in his loving, strong arms.

Is there a condition in your life that is troubling your mind? Or is there a Peninnah in your life whom you need to forgive? To Hannah, this situation demanded a divine intervention. For that reason, she desperately cried out to the Lord of heaven's armies, "Look upon my sorrow and answer my prayer and give me a son, then I will give him back to you. *He will be yours* for his entire lifetime" (1 Samuel 1:11, emphasis added). Wow! What a huge sacrifice Hannah made to God! She had come to a place of total surrender. I'm sure her offering touched God's heart. What about your sacrifice or offering? Are you feeling a tug in your heart to obey the Lord in some area of your life? Even now tell God in prayer.

Prayer

Lord, today I pour out all my heart's concerns to you. First, I choose to be obedient to you. I forgive everyone who has ever hurt me. Or if I have hurt others, I choose to make restitution. I have faith in you that you won't forget to answer my prayers. There is no God like you. You are supreme! Thank you for answering my prayers. Amen.

The Heavy Burden of Unforgiveness

In Genesis 37 we see a serious case of sibling rivalry; Joseph's brothers were jealous of him. One day when Joseph told his brothers about a dream he had, they became infuriated because they thought he was prideful and conceited. The situation grew even worse when Joseph had a second dream; this time he related to his brothers that "the sun, the moon, and the eleven stars bowed down to [him]!" (Genesis 37:9 NKJV).

Suddenly Joseph's brothers hated him so much that they started to think of ways to get rid of him. Isn't this a clear example of how hate starts to fester in our minds? It stays hidden deep inside us until the opportunity arises. One day when Joseph's father sent him to check on his brothers, who were in the fields pasturing the sheep, these guys suddenly started to make plans to kill him (Genesis 37:19–20). This may seem like a ruthless act, but hate and jealousy can give way to vicious and heartless thoughts, which can bring about fatal actions. Although we see Joseph's brothers changing their minds about murdering him, they still committed a terrible act of selling him to Midianite traders, who took him to Egypt (Genesis 37:28). There Joseph found himself all alone in a strange land separated from his family. How would you have responded if the people you really loved were spiteful and cruel toward you? I'm sure Joseph was brokenhearted and even confused about his brothers' attitude toward him.

Despite all the brutal actions Joseph had to endure, what I love about him is that he isn't moping and grumbling about his circumstances; nor is he seeking revenge. Instead, he served with diligence in the home of his Egyptian master, Potiphar (Genesis 39:1–6). What a commendable attitude to have!

What do you think was Joseph's secret in maintaining such a positive attitude? Do you think Joseph had already settled a few things between himself and God? Could it be that Joseph had to go before God, being honest and transparent about how he felt about the situation concerning his brothers? I believe Joseph had to deal with unforgiveness.

For a moment, let's think of some adjectives associated with forgiveness: compassionate, kindhearted, generous, merciful, understanding, tolerant, considerate, humane, and nice. Then let's think of adjectives related to unforgiveness: cruel, cold blooded, hard hearted, withholding good, merciless, spiteful, mean, resentful, envious, cutthroat, and unkind. Wow! Two altogether different lists.

I'm sure Joseph chose to be kindhearted, compassionate, and tolerant. Yes, I'm sure he was hurting, and he missed his family, but he had to come to a place of releasing that heavy burden of wrongdoing. He couldn't afford to think evil thoughts. He wanted to please God, so he worked hard and waited patiently for God to deliver him. Joseph's choice had to be forgiveness. If for some reason we find ourselves carrying unforgiveness, wallowing in anger, resentment, and bitterness, we need to release them. These are heavy burdens—like a debt we owe someone; these will weigh us down and depress us.

Jesus tells a beautiful story about forgiveness. The writer

gives an account of a debtor who owed a king ten thousand bags of gold, but he couldn't pay the money back, so *the king released him and forgave his debt.* But this same debtor, whom the king forgave for such a huge debt, refused to forgive his fellow servant, who owed him just one hundred silver coins. As a result, the servant was thrown into prison because the debtor demanded that the man pay up the full payment (Matthew 18:23–30 NIV).

This debtor didn't have mercy on his fellow servant. But Jesus, like the king, will always have mercy on us when we make a mistake. As we repent of our sins and turn to him, we can be sure God will never turn us away. He will forgive us. In the same way, when someone offends us, we need to forgive him or her.

For some people, forgiving someone isn't always easy. The offense might be so painful that they find themselves having a difficult time letting go of the memory of what happened in the past. Thank goodness, God knows all about those painful moments—how much they can disturb us. This is a good time to talk to God about all that's on your mind. Be honest and open minded with God. Remember, forgiveness is the very heartbeat of God. Even as we choose to forgive, God will walk us through and fill us with his love, which will enable us to forgive that person. At this very moment, the *healing process will begin.*

Is there someone who has hurt you in the past that you feel you need to forgive? According to 1 Corinthians 13: 4-5, "Love is patient and kind. Love is not jealous or boastful or proud or rude. It does not demand its own way. It is not irritable, and it keeps no record of being wronged." As you choose the path of forgiveness, God will surely give you a heart of love. Then you will be able to free yourself from any bitter feelings that may still be lingering in your heart. Even now as you pray, tell God the following:

Prayer

Dear God, I'm glad you don't keep a record of our wrongdoings; you forgive us. Right now, I surrender this situation, and I choose to forgive that person for hurting me. I refuse to keep a record of all the stuff that has happened in the past. Even now, I surrender everything to you. Amen.

69

Bring Your Issues to the King

Have you ever found yourself in a predicament that took you so much by surprise that you had to make a rash decision? It may have even put your life at risk, like what happened to Queen Esther. Through the book of Esther, we learn about the plight Esther suddenly found herself in. King Xerxes (Esther's husband) issued a decree that all Jews must be killed on a particular day—March 7 (Esther 3:12–13). Being a Jew, Queen Esther realized that even her life was in danger.

I'm sure Esther was disappointed and frustrated when she heard the news about what would befall her people. But she couldn't allow her feelings to get in the way. She had to do something positive, even daring. Esther knew it was time to approach the king. As she had hoped, when she made her entrance, the king welcomed her and held out the gold scepter to her (Esther 5:2). In the presence of the king, Esther requested that the lives of herself and her people be spared. Because of Queen Esther's petition, the king issued another decree. This time "the king's decree gave the Jews in every city authority to unite to defend their lives" (Esther 8:11).

Thank goodness Queen Esther brought this big issue to the king. Her courageous decision of "I will go in to see the king. If

I must die, I must die" (Esther 4:16) changed the entire dynamics of this situation. Only the king could have stopped this evil plot. *The king had the authority.* As it turned out, "on that day, the enemies of the Jews had hoped to overpower them, but quite the opposite happened. It was the Jews who overpowered their enemies" (Esther 9:1). Esther's daring decision to approach the king made it possible for the Jews to receive their deliverance.

Like Queen Esther, we need to bring our concerns to almighty God, the king of our lives, telling him, "How great is our Lord! His power is absolute! His understanding is beyond comprehension!" (Psalm 147:5). God is the one who is our number-one source of strength and help in the time of trouble.

We see that prior to being queen, Esther was hidden in the background. She wasn't popular until her beauty made room for her to become the queen. Because of that privilege, the king granted her much favor. She was able to ask for whatever she wanted and to seal it with the king's signet ring (Esther 8:8).

Like Queen Esther, we need to boldly approach King Jesus with our issues. The beauty about Queen Esther obtaining deliverance for herself and her people lies in the fact that *she didn't keep the issue to herself.* She "went again before the king, falling down at his feet and begging him with tears to stop the evil plot devised by Haman" (Esther 8:3). Esther approached the king, knowing that without his intervention, she and her people would be destroyed. Esther called on her people to fast and pray for three days. Note: she was neither quiet nor passive; she was desperate to see God intervene in her situation. In that hour of great need, when she turned to God, he didn't abandon her. God delivered her people from Haman's evil plot.

Esther was able to approach the king because of her status as queen. On what grounds do we approach God? As believers in Christ, we can confidently approach God because of the blood of Jesus. By his death, the blood of Jesus has opened up for us *a new and living way*. Now we can actually go right into the presence of God with sincere hearts—having our hearts cleansed from a guilty conscience (Hebrews 10:19–22 NIV). Yes, we now have access into the very throne room of God.

Like Esther we need to approach God with a tenacious attitude, knowing God desires to listen to us as we bring our issues to him.

What are some issues you might want to bring to God? Queen Esther brought a big issue to the king. Her position as Queen paved the way for her to obtain many privileges. As children of God, we have access to the throne room because our sins have been washed by the blood of Jesus. His blood has made it possible for us to receive all the promises and blessings God has provided for us. Right now, Jesus is seeing deep into our hearts and situations. He knows exactly how to deliver us, since his understanding of us is beyond human comprehension. That's the reason we need to cry out in prayer until the Lord breaks through. Tell God about your issue.

Prayer

Dear God, I choose not to be quiet or passive about this urgent issue looming in front of me. Because a new way is opened up for us through the blood of Jesus, I boldly approach you in prayer. I bring all the issues of my life to you. I humbly bow at the cross, where I know I will receive mercy and grace to help me in times of need. Thank you for your delivering power. Amen.

Shout a Bold Praise to God

All my life You have been so, so good … I will sing of
the goodness of God … you have led me through the
fire, And *in darkest night You are close* like no other.
—Jenn Johnson, "Goodness of God" (emphasis added)

Very often people find themselves crumbling under the pressure
of challenging circumstances, grief, and suffering—or heavy
workloads of too many assignments and tasks. In other cases,
people are so overwhelmed by their blunders or mistakes that
they find themselves rehearsing and dwelling on the past. So
there is no time for fun or enjoyment. No time for singing or
praising. No time for appreciating the goodness of God. Life
for them has become boring, dreary, and tedious.

During mundane times, we need to reach out to God. This is
a time for us to hear from God. A great way to know what God
is saying is by reading the Word. Isaiah 12 is a great chapter
to read. God has promised to be *our strength and song* (Isaiah
12:2 ESV). Instead of feeling discouraged or fearful, why not
shout a bold praise to God? I love how the writer bursts out in
exuberant praise to God, saying, "Sing praises to the Lord, for
he has done gloriously" (Isaiah 12:5 ESV). In down moments,

we need to see God is still working—our God is still mighty and wonderful; he is the one who will do glorious things for us.

When we find that we're having a difficult time expressing praise, a great place to start is by quietly saying, "Hallelujah" to God. This is the perfect word to say at this moment, because we are actually acknowledging that God deserves the highest note of praise. As we start to open up to God, the praise from our hearts will rise to our lips, and we can start to express how great and powerful God is.

One night, as I was listening to the song "How Great Thou Art," God ministered to me by letting me know that If I really did believe he was great, then I would trust him to help me with whatever task or challenge was before me. As we envision how great God is, let's start praising him for helping us with our daily chores, activities, and challenges, which may seem insurmountable at the moment. The next step we can take is by doing something positive. This will change our whole attitude about our circumstances.

One particular song I love to listen to is "Goodness of God" by Jenn Johnson. Jenn's song makes me know that God's goodness is running after me, not after my mistakes, wrong attitudes, problems, or failures. Because God is faithful, he will lead us even through the fire and the darkest night. Isn't this enough to make us know God hasn't forgotten us? He is right there with us to see us through every challenge—to give us the victory.

God wants to show us how great and powerful he is in every area of our lives. Let's not be afraid to let God in—especially in those moments when life looks like a big puzzle and the problem looks so huge that we have no clue as to how it will all end. This can be a nerve-racking moment, but it doesn't have to remain this way. This is the time to look into the Word. Tell

God, "You have given me the shield of your salvation, and your gentleness made me great ... you equipped me with strength for the battle" (2 Samuel 22:36, 40 ESV). As you hold on to his Word, God will surely give you the strength for this battle you're in. Because of God's faithfulness and lovingkindness toward his people, watch him come through for you.

Amid chaos and stress, how do you respond, or whom do you turn to? Do you believe God will work out each detail of this situation? The writer of Isaiah 12 chose to *shout a bold praise to God*, because he believed God did wonderful things for his people. He also asserted that he would trust God and not be afraid. As you begin to praise God, believe he is faithful, true to his Word, and that he is great and mighty. Acknowledging these qualities of God will lift the heaviness you have been carrying and fill you with a new song. Even now tell God the following:

Prayer

Today, I surrender all the tasks, assignments, and challenges to your hands. Even though I don't know which way to turn or the end results of this situation, I believe you are with me. You are my source of strength. Because of your help and faithfulness, you will see me through. In faith, I say, "Your goodness is running after me." Amen.

God in the Crisis

When you are in a crisis, you may feel many negative emotions—like fear, hopelessness, discouragement, doubt, loneliness, or anxiety. You may even find yourself in situations where you are trapped, threatened, or in financial lack. These dark circumstances can daunt our spirits and prevent us from moving forward spiritually, emotionally, and even physically. But this is the very moment for us to take refuge in God.

The chapters in "God in the Crisis" will further help you to navigate your way through these tough times until you see your breakthrough. In the meantime, don't lose hope but trust and wait for God to act on your behalf. As you will notice, some of the characters praised their way through, and others acted in obedience, while one woman chose to be sacrificial in her giving. Moreover, another woman was set free from an evil spirit, while one couple saw God perform a great miracle in their lives. As it turns out, God did a beautiful work in all their lives. Indeed, God showed up.

71

God, Our Refuge in Trouble

Are there times when you feel like you need to find someone to tell your deepest concerns to? When you can find no one, whom do you turn to? If this is the case, then you do have someone to turn to. Like David, you can cry out to God and pour out your complaints or troubles to him. God loves when we approach him with our issues, anxieties, and perplexities.

We envision David's deep heart cry in a time of trouble when he felt trapped by his enemies. David cried out to his God, "Rescue me from my persecutors, for they are too strong for me. Bring me out of Prison" (Psalm 142:6–7). He recognized that he was no match for his enemies; he wasn't strong enough. Like David, what in your life is causing you to feel vulnerable and imprisoned? In moments like these, how do you cope? Clearly, David demonstrates what we should do when we face adverse situations.

Like David, we need to *bring God into our situation* and allow him to handle it. When our emotions are going out of control, it's important for us to acknowledge that we need God; we can hide in him. Then we won't be easily shaken; God will hold us securely. He has our best interest in mind. In fact, he is a good God, not a bad heavenly Father, who is constantly on the lookout to punish his children because they are feeling frustrated or anxious about their situations.

God understands the negative emotions we are feeling; this is the perfect time for us to trust him with our circumstances. The psalmist David affirmed that "those who trust in the Lord will lack no good thing" (Psalm 34:10). When we go through bad situations and our paths look dark and scary, that's the time to depend on God. He promises that as we trust him, we will "lack no good thing." Yes, he wants to bless us with good things. However, many times our situation might be so bad to human eyes that we have a difficult time visualizing God's goodness. This is the time we need to remind ourselves of God's character. We can join with the psalmist and tell him, "You have become my rock of strength. Into your hands I now entrust my spirit. O Lord, the God of faithfulness, you have rescued and redeemed me … In mercy you have seen my troubles and you have cared for me; even during this crisis in my soul I will be radiant with joy, filled with praise for your love and mercy" (Psalm 31:4–7 TPT).

Note David's attitude in tough times. Because of David's close relationship with his God, he ran into the arms of God and poured out his complaints. He knew that when we are feeling caged in and vulnerable, the presence of God is a good place for us to go to. The writer instructs us, "Trust in him at all times, you people; pour out your hearts to him, for God is our refuge" (Psalm 62:8 NIV). The word *pour* gives the connotation of a soul that is thirsty for God—a soul that wants to let go to God, telling him the most treasured secrets of our hearts. God will listen to us and not turn his back on us. In other words, the presence of God is our "place of refuge." This is a place where we come face-to-face with a God who is mighty, strong, sufficient, and more than able to deliver us in times of trouble.

It's a place where God rejuvenates and comforts us so we can face the world with new strength and courage. During this time, our souls will find rest in God (Psalm 62:5).

In times of trouble, what is your expectation level like? God promises us that "those who look to him for help will be radiant with joy; no shadow of shame will darken their faces" (Psalm 34:5). God doesn't want our faces to be darkened with disappointment. As we learn to hide under the shelter of his everlasting arms, I believe God will rescue us from our troubles and fill us with joy.

At this moment, do you feel like pouring out your heart to God, telling him every single thing on your mind? Do you believe he will take care of this ordeal? As you begin to trust and obey him, tell God you're allowing him to lead you each step of the way until you see your deliverance. Like any good father, God is planning ahead of us to give us good things. He knows exactly what we need, even before we ask him. As you spend some time in prayer, tell God the following:

Prayer

Dear heavenly Father, I bring all my frustrations and anxiety to you. Today I choose to trust you instead of complaining about all the things troubling my mind. I choose to praise you in advance. I believe I will see your goodness and merciful hand in my life. Amen.

72

Trust God in Unpredictable Situations

The Lord directs the steps of the godly. He delights in every detail of their lives. Though they stumble, they will never fall!
—Psalm 37:23–24 ()

In unpredictable circumstances, we need to wholly lean on God to work out the details in our lives. At one time in my life, our family was faced with the decision of what to do concerning Mom's health. Mom had already been in the hospital for over seven weeks, and her health was rapidly declining. We were at the point where we weren't sure whether she would have to go to a rehabilitation center or go home to be in hospice care. Not only was it an emotional time for us, but there was much uncertainty about many details. Instead of worrying about what would be the outcome, our family knew we had to trust God to show us the right path to take. We couldn't depend on our finite understanding.

During that difficult time, I purposefully searched the scriptures for answers. God spoke to me through Matthew 10:29–31 (emphasis added), which says, "Not a single sparrow can fall to the ground without your Father knowing it. And the very hairs on your head are all numbered. So *don't be afraid*; you are more valuable to God than a whole flock of sparrows."

This verse reassured me that God wasn't just in the background of this situation, but he was in the forefront, orchestrating each aspect of the process.

At that point, although we didn't even feel or see how God would work, I took comfort in the fact that if our heavenly Father cared about every sparrow that fell to the ground, he must care about every phrase of this ordeal regarding Mom's well-being.

Like the sparrows, my mother is valuable in God's eyes. As it turned out, God showed up. He worked out every detail in a beautiful way that made us know that when we were going through rough situations, he was right there with us to help us and see us through.

Second Kings 4 gives an account of another woman who was in a desperate need for God to intervene. First, she had to deal with the death of her husband. Afterward, a creditor threatened to take her two sons away as slaves if she didn't pay up the debt her husband owed him (2 Kings 4:1 NIV). This situation made this woman go to the man of God, Elisha, who didn't turn her away.

I am sure Elisha understood the plight this woman was in. But he also knew a God who could turn her dilemma around, so he asked her, "How can I help you? Tell me, what do you have in the house?" (2 Kings 4:2 NIV). All this widow had was a small jar of olive oil. He instructed her to borrow as many empty jars as she could from neighbors and to pour the olive oil from her jar into the other jars. The prophet's instruction must have seemed impractical. But as her sons kept bringing jars to her, she was able to fill one jar of oil after another. Wow! Just one jar of oil was able to fill so many other jars. What a miracle God performed for this woman! (2 Kings 4:2–6 NIV).

Note: this woman brought to the prophet the only jar of oil

she had in her house. She didn't hold back. Her obedience and faith made it possible for her to have a bountiful supply of oil, which she was able to sell and pay her debt (2 Kings 4:7 NIV). Isn't it like God to take care of our need? I'm glad he didn't disappoint her. He came through at just the right time.

Isaiah 49:23 (NIV) encourages us, "Those who hope in [God] will not be disappointed." I'm glad God used Elisha to bless this widow. Like this woman, as we wait on God, he will come through for us. No matter how bleak or uncertain the circumstances may look, let's keep hoping, knowing that God will not fail us. He cares about each detail of our lives.

Are you concerned about a situation in your life? This woman's prompt obedience to the man of God brought about this miracle. Note: she didn't question his bizarre request. She did what he asked anyway. Can you picture her state of mind afterward when she saw how the oil multiplied? She knew she didn't have to worry anymore about her sons being carried off as slaves. She was able to sell the oil and pay the creditor. Yes, God did show up. He does care about each detail of our lives. Tell God you're believing him for a great ending as well. As you bow in prayer, say to God the following words:

Prayer

Lord, although the circumstances look dark, I choose to trust you. I won't let fear and doubt cloud my vision of how great and faithful you are. I commit all these concerns to you. I know you will help me, so I wait patiently for you to act because you are a never-failing God, who works out the details in our lives.

Trapped, but God Shows Up

Have you ever found yourself trapped in a situation where there seemed to be no way of escape? The situation or enemies around you may seem so powerful that fear started to step in. Isn't it comforting to know that when we are surrounded by fierce enemies, God doesn't leave us in our enemies' grip? His plan is always to deliver us.

Through 2 Kings 6, we see that the king of Aram was enraged because Elisha, the prophet, was constantly informing the king of Israel of all his actions. One morning when Elisha got up early and went outside, there were troops, horses, and chariots everywhere. The young man with him became afraid. Like many of us, he panicked, but Elisha was confident that God was right there with them (2 Kings 6:8–15).

The young man was viewing the situation from a human perspective. He couldn't see that God was on their side, so Elisha encouraged him and prayed that the Lord would open his eyes and let him see with a *new set of lenses.* The scripture records, "The Lord opened the young man's eyes, and when he looked up, he saw that the hillside around Elisha was filled with horses and chariots of fire" (2 Kings 6:17). Wow! Chariots of fire! This was God himself making his appearance. When

God is on our side, he doesn't leave us in a trapped or defeated situation. He comes to our rescue.

I can imagine how the young man's perspective changed when he saw the chariots of fire. How his fear changed to confidence! He then must have understood that God was on their side; he would be their help and rescuer. When the battle seems to be raging all around, he is right there with us in the middle.

Because the young man saw with a new set of lenses, he was able to witness the supernatural power of God right before his eyes. What's more amazing is that "as the Aramean army advanced toward him, Elisha prayed, 'O Lord, please make them blind.' So the Lord struck them with blindness as Elisha had asked" (2 Kings 6:18). Because of God's *divine* intervention in this situation, Elijah was able to lead the whole Aramean army in the wrong direction to the city of Samaria, where they had to plead for their lives. God turned the whole situation around, and his people were able to experience God's protective power.

Like the young man, we also need to see with a new set of lenses. Instead of letting fear and discouragement take over, we need to see our circumstances with the eyes of faith. Let's start believing we will see God's divine intervention in fierce battles and tough situations. In faith, start rejoicing because you know he will rescue you. Next, tell God, "I trust in your unfailing love. My heart rejoices in your salvation. I will sing the Lord's praise, for He has been good to me!" (Psalm 13:5–6 NIV). Indeed, this is a great moment to sing songs of praise to the Lord; be confident that he will show you his goodness.

God is sovereign; this means he has the power to work out any circumstance. No situation is too complicated or impossible for him to fix. With eyes of faith, let's declare that God will faithfully answer our prayers. Let's hope in him.

In those raging-storm moments or complicated situations, do you believe God is on your side and will help you? Isaiah 41:10 reminds us, "Don't be afraid, for I am with you. Don't be discouraged, for I am your God. I will strengthen you and help you. I will hold you up with my victorious right hand." This is a comforting promise. This means we don't have to go through life feeling all alone with no one to help us. God is right there with us to strengthen us and guide us to a safe, healthy, and thriving place. This is one of the benefits God's children can enjoy. As your faith in God rises, believe he will show up on your case. Let's start declaring the following:

Declaration

I declare God is more powerful than this battle raging all around me, so every weapon formed against me shall not succeed. I will now start to look out to see God's intervention in this situation. I am confident he will bring me out.

74

Praise God, Even When It Hurts

If you are fearful of something or someone, how do you deal with the situation? Some people pretend they aren't fearful, while others cave in, feeling disheartened, anxious, and uncertain. Because fear can daunt our spirits and prevent us from moving forward spiritually, emotionally, and even physically, we need to find a way to deal with it.

As we look at Psalm 116, our attention is drawn to a writer who is fearful of death, which seemed to be drawing near. He tells the Lord exactly how he feels by saying, "I am deeply troubled Lord. In my anxiety I cried out to you" (Psalm 116:10–11). Note: in the midst of what seems like a hopeless situation, the writer of this psalm still calls on the name of the Lord and praises God, telling him how kind, good, and merciful he is (Psalm 116:5). He doesn't let a negative situation prevent him from expressing and giving himself to God. He even asks a question: "What can I offer the Lord for all he has done for me?" (Psalm 116:12). Wow! How determined he is to acknowledge God's goodness!

Choosing to praise and give thanks is a decision we need to personally make. We can look at our troubles and complain and get depressed, or we can hold on to the promises of God.

Thanksgiving and praise have to be expressed. We cannot keep them inside us. Even when we're in a crisis or hurting physically or emotionally, we need to spend some time talking to God. It's a time when we offer a sacrifice of thanksgiving and call on the name of the Lord (Psalm 116:17). In this time of weakness, God will never turn us away, but he will comfort and strengthen us.

When we choose to make a sacrifice of praise or spend time worshipping God, we are actually honoring the Lord. These are precious moments. We will never come out the same. God will fill us with peace instead of worry, confidence instead of fear, joy instead of sorrow. Let's make this decision to praise, worship, and give thanks to God as long as we have breath.

When we are hurting and everything around us looks dark and unpromising, what is our response? I love how the writer of Psalm 34:1–2 (ESV) puts it: "I will bless the Lord at all times; his praise shall continually be in my mouth. My soul makes its boast in the Lord." The psalmist has definitely learned the secret of praising the Lord—not only in the good times but also when the situation doesn't look good. He knows this is the perfect time to trust God to come through for him. That's the time to take refuge in God, knowing he will *not* fail us.

Are you determined to still praise God, even though you can't see a way out of the situation? In these moments, when we praise and worship God, his heart will always be touched. Currently, what are some challenges you are facing? Note: God not only is pleased when we praise him in bad circumstances, but he actually inhabits our praises (Psalm 22:3 KJV). Yes, God will honor us with his presence, and we will enjoy peace, inner strength, and self-confidence. Even now, as you talk to God, praise him for his goodness and greatness.

Prayer

God, in the midst of this troubling situation, I want to tell you that although I am in so much pain, I will still praise you. I thank you for showing me your kindness and love. You have never failed me. I will praise and worship you as long as I have breath. Amen.

What a Breakthrough!

Cheer up! Take courage all you who love him. Wait for
him to break through for you, all who trust in him!
—Psalm 31:24 (TPT)

Have you found yourself in a position where you're longing to
see God breakthrough in your life? The circumstances around
you are causing you to become impatient, and you're even
starting to lose faith in God. You may even think God has
forgotten you or overlooked you.

In Genesis 30, we see Jacob's two wives, Leah and Rachel,
undergoing many struggles as women. While Leah craved
her husband's love and attention, Rachel longed to become
pregnant. Rachel watched her sister, Leah, getting pregnant
four times and giving birth to four sons. Eventually, she became
so jealous of her sister that she cried out to her husband, "Give
me children, or I'll die!" (Genesis 30:1 NIV). Rachel was
desperate about getting pregnant, but she couldn't see Jacob
wasn't responsible for her barrenness. Jacob had to sternly
remind her, "Am I in the place of God, who has kept you from
having children!" (Genesis 30:2 NIV). Rachel was so blinded
by her plight that she kept God out of her life.

Rachel had reached to a point where she was running out of

patience. She felt she must have children, so she told Jacob to sleep with her maid, Bilhah. Rachel hoped that through Bilhah, she could build a family to satisfy her maternal desire. Yes, her maid was able to give birth to two sons for Jacob. Maybe Rachel viewed these boys as her family (Genesis 30:4–7). She didn't see that God had something else in store for her. Something far more beautiful than what she had imagined. As always, God has the best in store for us.

Rachel couldn't see God's plan. After her servant girl gave birth to two children, she exclaimed, "I have had a great struggle with my sister, and I have won" (Genesis 30:7 NIV). For Rachel, this was like a game, a competition. Anytime we get into competition with others, God isn't in the mix—our eyes are either on ourselves or on the person we are competing with.

Rachel finally came to such a desperate place that she cried out to God, and God listened to her, and she gave birth to a son, Joseph (Genesis 30:22–23 NIV). Wow! God didn't turn his back on Rachel despite her many flaws of being jealous, blaming others and being in competition with her sister. God indeed showed Rachel how faithful and kind he is. Because of his unfailing love, he will always want to turn our disgrace to joy. He doesn't want us to stay in a state of disgrace or sorrow or in the place where we are continually walking in our mistakes. He wants to reveal himself to us. As we keep our eyes on him, he will show us his excellent plan for our lives.

Rachel may not have understood the plan God had for her son, Joseph. Little did she realize what a miracle child God had given her. How instrumental he would be in the hands of God!

Joseph went through many troubles (Genesis 37, 39–41). After his brothers threw him into a pit and afterward sold him to some Midianite traders, he found himself for many years in a strange land away from the family he loved. In Egypt,

Joseph could have blamed his brothers and complained about how unfair it was to be thrown into prison for a deed he hadn't done. Yet in all these situations, Joseph stayed faithful to God. How was Joseph able to cope with these antagonistic situations?

Joseph learned the secret of waiting on God. He understood what it meant to take refuge in his God. That's the place where we need to hide—depending on him when everything around us seems to be crumbling. Oh, how much we need God during this time! Taking refuge in God is a safe place to be in.

During those many years in prison, Joseph had to fully lean on God. We don't see Joseph whining about his circumstances, but he looked for opportunities to help others. When the chief cupbearer told him his dream, Joseph interpreted it, telling him the dream meant he would get out of prison. As it turned out, the dream did come to pass, so the cupbearer's former position was restored. Out of prison, the cupbearer forgot all about Joseph, but God didn't.

Our God will never forget about us—although sometimes it may seem that way.

Two years later, the Pharaoh of Egypt also had a dream no one could interpret. Finally, the cupbearer remembered Joseph had accurately interpreted his dream, so he told the king about him. Because Joseph was able to interpret Pharaoh's dream with much wisdom and precision, Pharaoh gave him the position of being second-in-command of the whole land of Egypt (Genesis 41:43 NIV). Wow! Joseph moved from a pit experience to a high position in the palace. What a breakthrough!

Isn't it amazing how much God cares about our affairs? Although we may never trace how God works, he does. As we see in Joseph's life, his obedience and confidence in God weren't wasted. And as always, God remains faithful.

Although Rachel and even Joseph didn't understand the

path God was taking them through, God was meticulously orchestrating all the events in their lives. God's plan is always greater than ours. When Joseph's brothers thought they were doing an evil act by throwing him in a pit and selling him, this was actually a setup by God himself. This was the perfect time for Joseph to be in Egypt. If he hadn't been in Egypt, he wouldn't have been able to save his entire family and many other lives (Genesis 50:20 NIV).

At times, do you find it difficult to understand God's ways? Although we might not be able to figure out what God is doing in many of our circumstances, we know his thoughts and ways are far higher than ours (Isaiah 55:8–9). Therefore, we need to look to God for guidance. In times of trouble, do you believe God is your fortress who will protect and deliver you? That's when we need to take refuge in him; it's a beautiful place to be in. I believe this is the place where Joseph found his strength and joy. As you trust him, are you committing everything to God and waiting patiently on him to work out those circumstances you can't control? Even now tell God the following:

Prayer

Lord, I bring this situation that is frustrating and even imprisoning me. Like Joseph, I won't lose faith, but I will put my trust in you. Because you are a faithful God, I will wait on you. I am confident you will break through in this situation. Amen.

Withholding Nothing

Have you ever found yourself in a financial crisis in which you didn't know what the outcome would be? At that point in your life, someone walked up to you and asked you to give him or her the same thing you were clearly in great need of. What would your attitude be like? Would you tell the person off, refuse to give what he or she was asking for, or complain that he or she was unreasonable? Let's see what the woman from Zarephath did when Elijah visited her and asked her for a meal during a very critical time in her life.

First Kings 17 recounts the story of the prophet Elijah visiting a widow in Zarephath during the time of a severe drought. From this woman's limited food supply, Elijah had the audacity, it would seem, to ask her to bring him a little water in a jar and a piece of bread. She told him that all she had in her house was a handful of flour and a little olive oil, which she was planning to use to make a meal for herself and son; afterward, they would both die (1 Kings 17:10–12). All this woman saw was a bleak, dark future of death awaiting her because of the circumstances she found herself in.

Thank goodness, amid a dilemma, there is still hope for positive change. Note, despite the circumstances, this woman didn't hold back from doing what the prophet had asked her to do. Little did she realize that what might have looked like a little favor touched God's heart.

In times of lack or dark moments when we can't see our way out and everything seems to be falling apart, we need to hear from God. This woman obeyed what the prophet had told her to do. Because of her generosity and her not-holding-back attitude, "there was food every day for Elijah and for the woman and her family. For the jar of flour was not used up and the jug of oil did not run dry, in keeping with the word of the Lord spoken by Elijah" (1 Kings 17:15–16 NIV). Wow, what a breakthrough! God does keep his promise; he will come through for us, even in a crisis.

This incident happened amid a drought season. As we see, she didn't know how she would get her next meal. Maybe this woman was praying to God; she was waiting expectantly for her miracle. Then the prophet showed up at just the right time. Isn't this how God works? Like this woman, we also might be cornered. Thank goodness God can make a way in any given situation. When there seems to be no possibilities or solution, he will surely find a way to bring us victoriously out. In the meanwhile, we need to hold on to the promises of God. Psalm 66:12 (NIV) reassures us, "We went through fire and water, but you [Lord] brought us to a place of abundance." Yes, in times of scarcity or if we find ourselves in a financial crisis, we need to believe God won't leave us in our broken condition, but he will bring us to "a place of abundance."

Note, the woman from Zarephath gave sacrificially. In the same way, we should give of our best—not complaining and holding back but with a loving and generous attitude. God is pleased when we give cheerfully. He will reward us in due time. In fact, when we take refuge in God and fear him, he promises we will *lack nothing* (Psalm 34:8–10 NIV). Because the woman from Zarephath gave willingly and took refuge in God, she tasted of the goodness of God.

In times of great need, do you believe that as you take refuge in God, you will "lack nothing"? Do you think this woman's trust in God made room for her miracle to take place? God loves when we put our trust in him rather than in man-made solutions. Trust starts from deep within as we take our eyes off the situation and keep our eyes on God. Then our heavenly Father, who knows exactly what to do in our situation, will work out all the details. Even now, let's start declaring that God will see us through.

Prayer

Lord, like this woman, I don't want to hold back anything you have asked me to do. I want to give with a willing and sacrificial heart, so Lord, lead me to someone to whom I can be a blessing. As I choose to put my trust in you and to have the right attitude, I know you will take care of my need—like you did for the woman from Zarephath. Amen.

Don't Lose Hope

Many times we find ourselves in disappointing situations. What we hoped would happen didn't happen, or at least it didn't happen immediately. That means we have no choice but to wait for the answer.

In Mark 2, four men anticipated bringing their paralyzed friend to Jesus; these men had hoped Jesus would pray for their friend and that he would immediately receive his healing. But when these men reached the house where Jesus was preaching the Word of God, it was so packed with people that there was no room left for them to get in (Mark 2:1–2 NKJV). Notice these men's attitudes: faced with a roadblock, these men didn't give up. What is our attitude when there's an obstacle in our way? Do we view the problem as being too big, or do we *still pursue our miracle*?

For a moment, let's take a look at the attitude of these four men. The problem was right before their eyes; there was no way these men could have gotten inside the house to where Jesus was. It was impossible for them to squeeze through the crowd to get to Jesus, yet these men refused to lose hope. As a matter of fact, they came up with a daring plan. They uncovered the roof of the house, which wasn't even theirs. Then they let their friend down through the roof (Mark 2:3–4 NKJV). I can imagine how surprised the crowd was to see a man burst through the roof and land right in front of Jesus.

Jesus saw how determined these men were to see their friend get his healing. Because of their faith in Jesus, these men were able to see a miracle happen right before their eyes. Even though some of the people in the crowd were criticizing Jesus, the air was still filled with faith and expectancy. These four men weren't focusing on the negative attitude of the other people in that room. They were confident Jesus would perform a miracle.

Turning to the paralyzed man, Jesus said, "I say to you, arise, take up your bed, and go to your house.' Immediately he arose, took up the bed, and went out in the presence of them all" (Mark 2:11–12 NKJV). What a miracle! What faith these men demonstrated! In the midst of criticism, obstacles, or setbacks, what is our response? Although these men didn't get their answer right away, they were determined, hopeful, and patient; these are three great characteristics to show when things don't seem to be working out. As a result, God finally came through for them. Their perseverance and waiting paid off.

The Israelites also had to wait for their breakthrough, but they had to wait a long time. They were living in Egypt for 430 years, working as slaves there (Exodus 12:40). Not only was the physical labor they were involved in tedious and uncomfortable, but I can picture them being emotionally and mentally drained. Under these unpleasant and uncomfortable circumstances, tears flowing down their faces, their cries went up to heaven. These people worked year after year, hoping God would deliver them.

These Israelites were God's chosen people, whom God deeply cared for. He saw how much they were suffering, so he said, "I have surely seen the oppression of my people who are in Egypt, and have heard their cry because of their taskmasters, for I know their sorrows. So I have come down to deliver them out of the hand of the Egyptians, and to bring them up from that land to a good and large land, to a land flowing with milk and honey" (Exodus 3:7–8 NKJV). Yes, they underwent much frustration, pain, and suffering. They must have even felt that God had forgotten about them. But all the while, God was looking on. As always, God's timing is perfect, but sometimes it doesn't look that way. If this is the case, what is your response? Are we patient, or are we complaining about how unfair God is? Maybe you are in a predicament, and you're asking yourself, *How can God do this to me?* Thoughts like these can cross our minds. But that's the time for us to lean on God. God will give us his grace to keep us from stumbling and falling to pieces.

The situation of the Israelites looked dark and hopeless as they "continued to groan under their burden of slavery. They cried out for help, and their cry rose up to God. God heard their groaning" (Exodus 2:23–24). Isn't it beautiful to know their cries finally "rose up to God"? When our prayers look as if they are just hitting the ceiling and bouncing back, we need to *continue to persevere.* God will eventually hear our deep heart cry! Thank goodness "[God] looked down on the people of Israel and knew it was time to act" (Exodus 2:25). I'm glad God didn't leave the Israelites in their disappointment and struggles; he came through for them.

The Lord kept his promise and "brought the people of Israel out of the land of Egypt like an army" (Exodus 12:51). Isn't this like God? He looks down and sees our heartaches and deep hurts. He doesn't want to leave us in our pain or sorrow. He shows up! As always, we can count on God's miraculous hand to rescue us.

Are you believing God for a breakthrough or miracle in your life? Note: the paralyzed man received his miracle because of his friends' persistence. His healing made it possible for them to see an amazing miracle. They had the opportunity to see God's power at work right before their eyes. Similarly, the Israelites experienced God's miraculous power. Although they had waited for so many years, God didn't abandon them; he revealed his powerful hand to them. Right now, if it appears as if God isn't answering your prayers, don't despair. Keep persevering until he shows up. Let's start declaring that our miracle is on the way.

Declaration

Lord, despite all the obstacles lying in my path, I won't give up. I will keep praying, believing, and looking for this miracle. I know you are a prayer-answering God, a Healer, and a Deliverer.

78

The Long Wait Is Over

The story of Elijah and the rain in 1 Kings 18 has not only captured my imagination but also made me see that God still works when it seems like nothing is happening. The people of Israel had been experiencing a period of a long drought. Those years of waiting for rain to come must have been exasperating for them. Thank goodness that in dark moments, God still shows up.

In the third year of the drought, the Lord told Elijah to go to King Ahab and tell him he would send rain. Can you picture Elijah's reaction? This had to be great news for him. This was a promise from God himself. Elijah could have said, "The Lord promised me this, so he is bound to fulfill his Word. I can now go home and sleep, or do something fun and exciting." Instead, "Elijah climbed to the top of Mount Carmel and bowed low to the ground and prayed with his face between his knees" (1 Kings 18:42).

Elijah acknowledged God's Word and did something about it; he prostrated himself before God and continued to pray. He was praying that God's Word would come to pass. What's our response when God gives us a Word?

Note, Elijah not only prayed but also *waited expectantly*

on God to answer his prayer. He knew he was praying to a God who honors his Word. The Bible tells us, "The word of the Lord is right and true; He is faithful in all He does" (Psalm 33:4 NIV). God's character is unblemished. For that reason, we can put our hope in him, knowing he will not fail us. That's the kind of faith Elijah had in God, a faith that was so strong and unwavering that he was confident God would answer his prayer. Believing God would do what he had said he would do, Elijah waited for him to answer.

For a moment, let's imagine this scene between Elijah and his servant.

Elijah: Go. Look toward the sea. See if there is any sign of rain coming.

Servant: Master, the sky is clear. There is absolutely no sign of rain.

Elijah: Look again. I've been praying for this to happen for a long time. I believe we will soon see rain.

Servant: Sorry, Master, again I looked. There is still no sign of rain.

Elijah: Keep looking. Don't get weary looking. Believe that God will answer us.

Servant: Master, this is already the third time. There is still no sign of rain. It looks like it won't happen. We're going to be in this drought condition forever. Forever! Then what will happen to us?

Elijah: Don't panic. Remember, God spoke it. It's got to happen. Keep your hopes high. And keep your eyes on God.

Servant: Master, again I looked. I'm telling you ... there is no sign of rain. No sign! I am starting to get tired and discouraged.

Elijah: I know you've already gone out to sea four times. But don't give up. *We have to be determined about pursuing what God has promised us.* Even if it looks like it's not happening, we still have to believe God's Word. Expect it will happen. Not because our prayer doesn't get answered right away - God has disappointed us. We need to keep praying. Keep staying on our knees. Keep believing. *We will see answers!*

Servant: I heard what you said about pursuing God, but why is it taking so long? Everything is still the same. Nothing has changed.

Elijah: Know one thing—*what God promises must come to pass!* We are too close to seeing God fulfill his promise. This time go out to sea with a new expectancy. Dream it, envision the answer, and watch how quickly God will bring the answer.

Servant: Master, this is the sixth time I've gone out, but I still didn't see anything. I intently looked north, south, east, and west. But there was no indication of rain in the sky. But I admit, this time something is different. I feel new hope—a longing to see God move. Even now, I'm envisioning this miracle. I believe a breakthrough is about to take place.

Elijah: Yes! I do sense new faith rising up in your heart. Well, we can't afford to stop believing now! *We are at the brink of seeing a miracle.* You need to keep looking until it happens. Start smelling it, feeling it, prophesying about it, and writing about it. God says it, so it's bound to happen. God cannot fail.

Servant: [Excitedly] Master, it's happening! Just like you said! I saw a sign—a little cloud about the size of a man's hand rising from the sea.

Elijah: Yes! I know God cannot fail. Now hurry and tell King Ahab the rain is coming!

Just as Elijah had expected, "soon the sky was black with clouds. A heavy wind brought a terrific rainstorm" (1 Kings 18:45).

Prayer

God, although it may look like our prayers are taking so long to get answered, we will *not* give up. We entrust our prayer requests, dreams, struggles, relationships, and conflicts to your hands. God, I believe you will come through for us. Amen.

79

Set Free from an Evil Spirit

When you're going through infirmity or pain, how do you expect people to react to you? Are there many stipulations about when and how you should receive your healing? In some cases, the people around you might view your situation with critical eyes, so matters can get out of hand. But even in these circumstances, God can show up and change the whole picture.

As recorded in Luke 13, some people weren't expecting Jesus to heal at that particular time. As a matter of fact, the ruler of the synagogue, where Jesus was teaching, was indignant that Jesus had healed on the Sabbath day (v. 14). Right in that synagogue, there was "a woman who had a spirit of infirmity eighteen years, and was bent over and could in no way raise herself up" (Luke 13:11 NKJV). Can you imagine the discomfort and pain this woman was experiencing from day to day for eighteen years?

When Jesus looked at this woman, he was immediately moved with compassion. Isn't this like Jesus? He understands our pain and aches, and he wants to do something about them. For that reason he called the woman over and said to her, "'Woman, you are loosed from your infirmity.' And He laid His hands on her, and immediately she was made straight, and glorified God" (Luke 13:12–13 NKJV). This woman was so overjoyed that she praised God for showing her such favor.

Can you picture the expression on this woman's face when suddenly her back was straightened and she could walk normally? When this woman first walked into the temple, I believe she didn't realize this would be her day for a miracle. In times of sicknesses, let's always be open minded. Let's see that healing is one of the privileges of God's children; as a child of God, we have a right to receive our healing at any time and in any place. Even when people don't believe we should receive our healing, we shouldn't lose faith.

Expectation plays a great part in receiving our miracle. Although negative circumstances might look as if God isn't answering our prayer, they shouldn't determine the outcome of the situation. In the midst of what seems like a bad report, we need to keep our eyes on God and still be in a hopeful attitude. Simply, we need to trust God wholly for the results.

When Jesus encountered this woman, he couldn't let her stay in her bondage. He had to set her free. According to Isaiah 61:1, Jesus has been sent "to comfort the brokenhearted, and to proclaim that captives be released, and prisoners will be freed." It is no wonder when Jesus saw this woman was oppressed by Satan, his heart was touched.

Jesus's mission on earth is to set the captives free. Any form of enslavement or addiction will always catch Jesus's eyes, because he knows how detrimental this is to people's well-being. Enslavement prevents us from moving forward. But when Jesus comes on the scene of our hearts, change takes place. Miracles happen.

Even the outraged voices of the religious people couldn't stop Jesus from healing this woman held in bondage. They were doubters. And doubters have no expectancy or faith that God will work miraculously. This means we don't fix our eyes on doubters, dream killers, critics, or anyone who will weaken our faith. We fix our eyes on God, our Healer—the one who wants to change situations from bad to good and to extraordinary.

In bad circumstances, how hopeful are you? What are you expecting God to do in this situation where you find yourself? At this moment, if you don't have a hopeful or positive attitude, don't be discouraged. One way we can change our attitude is by reading the Word of God and listening to songs that speak of God's greatness and faithfulness. In this way faith will start to rise within us to believe God for this miracle we are praying for. According to the psalmist, God "forgives all [our] sins and heals all [our] diseases" (Psalm 103:3 NIV). This is a great scripture to proclaim when we are believing God to see a breakthrough for any form of sickness or disease. Even now let's start declaring the following:

Declaration

With much expectancy, I am looking out to see a manifestation of God's healing power. You are a miracle-working God, who wants to heal *all* our diseases. I declare I will receive healing for this disease. Amen.

80

Let Amazing Take Place

Amazing grace! Amazing healing! Amazing peace! Amazing joy! Amazing love! Amazing God! Amazing goodness! Amazing ...

Do you sometimes want to see something amazing take place? Maybe you have been hoping to see a miracle happen right before your eyes. One important characteristic of God is his amazing goodness, which he continues to demonstrate. The writer asserts, "How great is the goodness you have stored up for those who fear you ... blessing them before the watching world" (Psalm 31:19).

One evening my heart was stirred to see God move in an extraordinary way. So much was on my mind that I knew I had to turn to an amazing God, who I know does amazing things. Through Psalm 86:10, we are reminded that God is great and does marvelous deeds. He alone is God. This promise encourages us to believe God will show up in many areas of our lives.

As hard as we might try to visualize how God would work, we will never cognitively understand. That's because God's thoughts and ways are far higher than ours (Isaiah 55:8–9 NIV). Although we may never fathom how God does his amazing work, one thing we know for sure is that we can trust him with all our issues. God is a Good Father, who is full of compassion. He will never abandon his children or turn away from them when their hearts are broken, discouraged, or impatient.

At other times, the miracle God has promised to perform seems to be taking too long to come to fruition. But that's the very time God wants us to wait patiently on him. In Psalm 138: 8, the psalmist cries out, "The Lord will work out his plans for my life—for your faithful love, O Lord, endures forever. Don't abandon me, for you made me." Yes, God is concerned about every one of our plans. Although we might not know how it will all work out, we do know he works in amazing ways far beyond our comprehension. We can be assured that each phase of our lives and *each issue on hand are on God's agenda.*

I think of the amazing story of Abraham and Sarah in the book of Genesis. When Abraham was seventy-five years old and Sarah was sixty-five, God promised that his wife would give birth to a son. However, Sarah, realizing she was already too old, inwardly asked, "How could a worn-out woman like me enjoy such pleasure, especially when my master—my husband—is also so old?" (Genesis 18:12). To the human eyes, it may look like God had forgotten about his promise. While Sarah doubted the promise of God, Abraham still held onto it.

Looking back at Abraham's life, we see that he made a huge mistake by impregnated Sarah's servant, Hagar, and giving her a son (Genesis 16:15). Notice: despite Abraham's flaw, God didn't withhold his blessing from him. I am sure Abraham repented of his sin, and God had mercy on him. From there onward, Abraham faithfully followed God's ways. His relationship with God mattered.

Abraham knew God was faithful; he would fulfill what he had promised. For that reason, he couldn't keep his eyes on Sarah's body; his eyes had to be on God. I am sure Abraham observed Sarah's body getting weaker and older. But because Abraham believed God's word, he waited patiently for many years for this promise to come to pass. Finally, Sarah conceived and bore Abraham a son in her old age. So when Sarah was ninety years old and Abraham was one hundred, God fulfilled his promise. And at just the time when God had said it would happen, their son, Isaac, was born (Genesis 21:3–5). Isn't this like our God to keep his word?

Abraham did not forget the promise God had given him. What about the promise God gave you? Does it seem too impossible for it to come to pass? Look at Sarah. God literally had to heal Sarah's dead womb. God is an expert at changing our body structure and even our hormone level to perform an amazing miracle.

Do you believe our God is the God of great wonders and awesome power? Do you think it will make a difference if we let God into our situations so he can work out his plan for our lives? As faith starts to rise in your heart, tell God, "You are the amazing God of creation who is able to heal our bodies and fix anything that looks impossible and hopeless." God, you keep your word! Because you demonstrated your awesome power in Abraham's life, I choose to trust you with this impossible situation at hand.

Prayer

Thank you for your perfect, steadfast, and unfailing love toward us. Because of your amazing love, I know I can trust you. First, I need to change my mindset so I can see you are the Creator God who can do anything. Like Abraham, I will keep my eyes on you until I see my miracle come to pass.

The Battles We Face

Whether a battle is fierce or mild, we can become so absorbed with the conflict or fight that we can lose sight of the solution. When we are in a battle, we are fighting an enemy—within or without; either way, we can become fearful, discouraged, vulnerable, or angry. But are we going to let all these negative emotions build up? The belief that "the human spirit is resilient" is indeed true for every single battle we will ever face. This means our minds have the potential to instinctively shift to "overcoming mode" rather than to dwell on thoughts of defeat and failure. This is the moment when we need to think of a strategy. The chapters in "The Battles We Face" will therefore show us how to overcome some of these everyday struggles, such as temptation, anger, obstacles in our path, the bondage of sin, and also feelings of unworthiness. These readings convey that God, our mighty Warrior, will fight with and for us in each situation and every season. As we surrender our lives to him, he'll make a way and equip us with strength and power, and fill our hearts with joy and singing.

81

In Fierce Battles, Sing in Faith

—I'm gonna to sing in the middle of a storm … my
weapon is my melody, Heaven comes to fight for me.
—Melissa and Jonathan Helser, "I Raise
a Hallelujah" (emphasis added)

When faced with a battle, what is your reaction? Do you run and
hide, and get anxious and fearful? If that happens, God won't
condemn you. In 2 Chronicles 20, even King Jehoshaphat was
alarmed when he heard a vast army was approaching them. So
"Jehoshaphat resolved to inquire of the Lord, and he proclaimed
a fast for all Judah. The people of Judah came together to seek
help from the Lord; indeed, they came from every town in
Judah to seek him" (2 Chronicles 20:3–4 NIV). Note: although
at first Jehoshaphat was terrified, he chose to seek the Lord's
help, declaring that the God of his ancestors was the ruler of
all the kingdoms of the earth; he is powerful and mighty, and
no one can stand against him! (2 Chronicles 20:6) Yes, when
situations or people come against us, we need to declare that
our God is powerful and mighty. He has the power to take care
of those enemies. Like Jehoshaphat, we need to acknowledge
that "no one can stand against our God."

I am glad Jehoshaphat went before God in prayer. He didn't

give in to fear. Being fearful in a battle just makes the situation worse. Fear is an emotion that will overwhelm or even bewilder us to the point that we can lose sight of God.

In a battle, our eyes need to constantly be on God. Because Jehoshaphat realized this truth, he declared that when his ancestors were faced with a calamity, they cried out to God, and he heard their prayers and saved them (v. 9). When we acknowledge that God delights to hear our prayers and rescue us, fear diminishes, and our view of God changes. We start to believe our God is big and powerful, and our enemies are little and weak.

As our eyes are fixed on the Lord, he will tell us what our next move should be. In a fierce battle, we need to hear a word from the Lord. On this occasion, the word came through Jahaziel, the son of Zechariah, who said to the people, "Do not be afraid or discouraged because of this vast army. For *the battle is not yours, but God's* … you will not have to fight this battle. Take up your positions; stand firm and see the deliverance the Lord will give you … The Lord will be with you" (2 Chronicles 20:15, 17 NIV, emphasis added).

Wow! I believe this affirmation changed their perspective of the situation and God. They came to realize that the battle was God's, not theirs. God was right there, fighting for them. This understanding must have changed their attitude—from being fearful to becoming courageous.

After hearing those prophetic words from Jahaziel, I am sure the people's expectations rose to another level. The instruction to "stand firm and see the deliverance the Lord will give you" was so well received that King Jehoshaphat and all the people bowed low with their faces to the ground. The Word from the Lord brought them to a place of worship (v.18).

In worship, self is dethroned, and we fix our eyes on God.

Then we can take our position—of standing firm, waiting, and watching in faith until we see the Lord's victory. God knows that as human beings we tend to get frustrated or flustered, but God wants us to carefully listen to all his commands and not take matters into our own hands.

Because of the king's faith in God, he appointed singers to walk ahead of the army. As they began to sing and praise God, they won a mighty victory (2 Chronicles 20:21–23). This was a powerful demonstration of God's power. God is pleased when we sing praises to him, even before the victory is won.

What are some songs we can sing? I was writing up this devotional when I decided to go on YouTube. Guess what popped up on my screen? It was this song, "I Raise a Hallelujah." I clicked on it, and Melissa's strong, anointed voice roared, "I'm gonna to sing in the middle of a storm … my weapon is my melody, Heaven comes to fight for me." Wow, was I excited, especially since I was writing and reading about singing in the middle of a battle.

Yes, our singing is a melody—a weapon against the enemy. In the middle of a storm/battle, as we sing *in faith*, heaven will certainly fight for us. In fact, the Lord honors his people when they praise him, even when they can't see a speck of hope in the situation.

You should never underestimate those moments when you are *singing in faith*—when your prayers aren't yet answered or you're in the middle of painful experiences. God is taking note of your trust in him. He is pleased when we sing in faith. It is no wonder that God was on Jehoshaphat's side, and they won a great victory that day. Yes, they defeated that vast army through seeking God's help, declaring how great and mighty he is, singing praises to almighty God, and being obedient to God's instructions.

Are you in a battle right now? Like Jehoshaphat, we need to come to the place where we say, "We do not know what to do, but our eyes are on you" (2 Chronicles 20:12 NIV). What a confession! Our eyes being on God makes all the difference. In the middle of a battle, what kind of thoughts are filling your mind? You can tell yourself, "I will not be afraid! I will not be discouraged. The battle is not mine; it's God's." When we don't see the miracle we are praying for, *let's still keep on singing about the unfailing love of God!* Singing is one of the most beautiful expressions of praise to God. So let's never stop singing praises to him.

Praise Moment

Lord, in the middle of this battle, struggle, storm, I choose to sing a new song to you. You have done wonderful things for me in the past, so why should I allow discouragement to take over? I choose to keep my eyes on you and not on the problem. I believe through you I will win a great victory.

Entrapment of the Soul

Therefore, my beloved, run [keep far, far away]
from [any sort of] idolatry [and that includes
loving anything more than God, or participating in
anything that leads to sin and enslaves the soul].
—1 Corinthians 10:14 (AMP)

The apostle Paul cautioned us about idolatry—to "flee from the
worship of idols" (1 Corinthians 10:14). The Amplified Bible
takes this idea of worshipping idols a little further by saying
that idolatry also "includes loving anything more than God."
This means you can love an activity, something, or a person
to the point that it is actually drawing you away from God
and leading you into sin. Without realizing it, that person is
enslaving his or her soul.

The writer of Isaiah 55:2 asks, "Why spend your money
on food that does not give you strength? Why pay for food that
does you no good?" Every person at some point of his or her life
may eat food that isn't healthy. Not only do we waste money, but
it doesn't give us the right nutritional value we need to maintain
a healthy body. Yet we still find ourselves eating unhealthy
food. In the same way, we can get so absorbed in activities that
don't build us spiritually that little by little they start to take

over our lives, leaving us enslaved and unfulfilled. As a matter of fact, they entrap us. What follows is regret and guilt, which blocks our hearts from truly worshipping God.

Just like God, who loves to free you from any enslavement, his voice calls out, "Listen, and you will find life" (Isaiah 55:3). As we start to open our hearts to what God is saying, he will lead us step by step so we can have a life full of purpose and meaning. Definitely, God doesn't want to leave his people chained to bad habits, strongholds, or bad behavioral patterns. He wants to beautify our lives.

As the Creator, God knows every single thing about our lives. "From his throne [the Lord] observes all who live on the earth. He made their hearts, so he understands everything they do" (Psalm 33:14–15). God understands us through and through, even to the very intents of our hearts. Therefore, our very souls are open to God. Naked! Nothing about ourselves can be hidden from him. And nothing is too far gone that he can't fix or too messed up that he can't heal. In fact, *God's love language to us* is, "Come to me with your ears wide open" (Isaiah 55:3). This is God's invitation to us. Can you picture God's welcoming arms stretched out toward you? Not to condemn you but to deliver you. And to make you whole.

As we start to reflect on our own lives, what are some of the things that can entrap us? Pornography, sex, drugs, smoking, video games, alcohol, money? The list goes on. At this moment, do you feel like something has been captivating your mind to such an extent that when you're in contact with it, you can't think sensibly? You find out that you can't free yourself from that bondage? It's too strong to resist. However, you want to be set free.

Before Jesus' death on the cross, we were captives of sin; our sinful nature wasn't yet cut away. However, Jesus' purpose for dying on the cross was to deliver us from our sinful nature. Our sinful nature is what keeps us in bondage. However, God in his love and mercy toward us has set us free from the slavery of sin, so he has canceled any record of those sins by nailing them to the cross (Colossians 2:13–14). This means that as we choose to walk in God's path, God will forgive us for *all* our sins and give us a brand-new nature. In fact, "God declared *an end to sin's control* over us by giving his Son as a sacrifice for our sins" (Romans 8:3, emphasis added). Jesus's great sacrifice of dying on the cross for us has set us free from the entrapment of sin.

We in our human finite strength can never free ourselves from this heavy weight of sin. Thank goodness Jesus has made a way for us. As we come to him with our weary and burdened hearts, we will find *rest for our souls* (Matthew 11:28–29). This rest Jesus promised is our privilege; this is granted to us through the Holy Spirit—our Comforter, Advocate, Intercessor, Counselor, Strengthener, and Standby (as seen in the next devotional).

Do you feel burdened by the entrapment of sin to the point that you want to make a change? As you surrender your life to God, decide to walk in God's path. Flee evil desires and pursue righteousness. Then watch how God will help you to escape the trap of the devil (2 Timothy 2:22–26). As you turn to God, he will have mercy on you, forgive your sins, and give you the strength and power to overcome all that once kept you enslaved. As you surrender your life to God, he will heal your soul. Now, instead of being burdened down with sin, it's possible for you to leave the old paths of sin and walk in righteousness.

Commitment

Lord, today I turn from my old ways; I am no longer a slave to sin, but I choose to follow the path of righteousness. Instead of wasting my time on pleasurable things that don't enhance or fulfill my life, I change direction. Through you, I am confident that I will find joy, peace, and rest for my soul.

83

Identify and Overcome

How in the world can we overcome a weakness we haven't identified? Maybe someone even brought up that area of vulnerability, and you told him or her, "Sorry, that's not my weakness. I'm over that!" In other words, you just brush it aside or simply act as if it isn't there. Let's see how the apostle Paul dealt with a particular weakness in his life.

The Apostle Paul's words enlighten us about the great revelations he received from God. However, he acknowledges that he was given a thorn in the flesh, a messenger from Satan to torment him and keep him from becoming conceited (2 Corinthians 12:7). Although Paul viewed this as an enemy who had caused him much pain, be believed God had allowed this battle in his life to keep him humble and steadfast in his faith.

Like all humans, I am sure he was uncomfortable with this "thorn in the flesh." The mere fact that Paul pleaded with the Lord three times to take away this weakness shows he was conscious of it; he preferred that this wouldn't be part of his life (2 Corinthians 12:8). Notice, he didn't sweep it under the carpet. Nor did he pretend it wasn't there, but he identified it and chose to deal with it by bringing it to the Lord.

Paul understood that God was concerned about every

single battle we might be going through more than we can ever imagine. He knew it was important to bring up any "thorn in the flesh" issue to the Lord. Thankfully, God gave Paul an answer. He told him, "My grace is sufficient for you, for my power is made perfect in weakness" (2 Corinthians 12:9 NIV). More than ever, Paul had to hold on to this truth that there was a greater power at work in his life. That power is the Holy Spirit. When we surrender those weak areas to the Lord, we are actually giving God a chance to work with us so we can receive his grace—his power to overcome those vulnerable areas in our lives. If we try to overcome any weakness or flaw in our own finite strength, we will always feel incapable and powerless. We need to depend on the Holy Spirit. He is our Helper, who will be to us our Comforter, Advocate, Intercessor, Counselor, Strengthener, and Standby (John 16:7 AMP).

- Your Comforter: Think of someone bringing you comfort and consoling you in that moment when you feel you have failed the Lord or feel distraught or discouraged. The Holy Spirit will encourage and motivate you not to give up; he wants you to run after God with diligence so you can accomplish his purpose.
- Your Strengthener: You feel vulnerable, but he comes over to you and picks you up like a strong, loving daddy would. Suddenly, you feel strong and full of power to overcome that weakness or ordeal.
- Your Intercessor: In the garden of Gethsemane, Jesus prayed not only for himself but also for the whole human race. Even now, Jesus is personally interceding for you. He is watching over your soul so you will not go astray but do the Father's will.

- Your Counselor: Think of a therapist. He or she wants to help you understand what's going on deep inside. In the same way, the Holy Spirit understands and connects with your emotions—the questions on your mind, the fear about the future, and even that particular area of weakness. God won't deal harshly with you, but he will find a way to help you resolve the issues deep inside.
- Your Advocate: The Holy Spirit inside you will be your greatest supporter and encourager. He will have your back in all circumstances. He will not forsake you. He will give you a new inner strength and vitality in every situation.
- Your Standby: He will serve as a standby in thick and thin. In every place you go and in every situation you're in, he will cover you. He will be standing by right there to assist you and to intervene so you don't fail or fall apart.

We all need the above attributes of the Holy Spirit in our lives on an everyday basis. Paul allowed the mighty power of the Holy Spirit to work in him. He knew that through him, *he would be able to accomplish* infinitely more than he could ever ask or think (Ephesians 3:20).

How do you deal with weaknesses or roadblocks that are tormenting or defeating you? Paul realized he couldn't deal with the challenges of life in his own human strength; *it's a faith walk!* He had to depend on the Holy Spirit to fight for him. Paul knew all of heaven was backing him. Instead of being petrified or wondering how it would all turn out, he was confident that his God would stand with him. In a fight or battle, we don't fight with human weapons like swords, spears, or javelins. But we lean on God, our helper and shield. Paul learned to keep his eyes on God and to depend on the Holy Spirit. That's how we overcome a weakness.

Prayer

Dear God, I bring this "thorn of the flesh," which has been causing so much stress and discomfort in my life. Thank you for this new revelation of who you are to me. Now I believe you will stand with me and rescue me. Thank you for the Holy Spirit, my Helper, who is my Comforter, Advocate, Intercessor, Counselor, Strengthener, and Standby. He is with me at all times. You will help me to overcome every weakness. Amen.

84

Sin Has Lost Its Power

Have you ever wondered what really happens when people say they have given their hearts to Jesus? Many Bible teachers refer to the "old nature" as our past, old sinful self before we decided to surrender our lives to Jesus. After conversion or when we give our hearts to Jesus, we receive the "new nature," signifying that our hearts are changed, and we now desire to please our heavenly Father.

Because of Jesus's death on the cross of Calvary, "we know that our old sinful selves were crucified with Christ so that sin might lose its power in our lives. We are no longer slaves to sin" (Romans 6:6). The writer is actually saying we have the privilege of receiving the "new nature," which is the Holy Spirit living in our hearts to strengthen and help us from day to day to live a victorious life. This doesn't mean we will never have to deal with sin anymore; occasionally the old sinful nature still pops up. That's the devil showing up to tempt us.

Once we are saved, the devil will never leave us alone. The devil's plan is to entice us so we will fall into sin again.

Because of Adam and Eve's sin in the garden of Eden, the devil had once enslaved us, but Jesus's death on the cross freed us from the bondage of sin. Adam and Eve were created to enjoy the presence of God and to live sin-free lives. But when the devil came along, they gave in to his temptation by eating the fruit from the tree God had forbidden them to eat. Afterward, they felt so ashamed that they hid from God by covering themselves with fig leaves (Genesis 3:7–8 NIV). Note: sin will always cause us to hide from God. We can never boldly go into the presence of God with sin in our hearts.

Because of Adam and Eve's sin, they were thrown out of the garden of Eden, but God didn't stop loving them. He still cared for them and mankind. *He cares about our souls.*

What is your soul contending with? Or what is pulling at your heartstrings to such a point that your heart is pulling you away from the very person and things you cherish most? Maybe you had purposed in your heart that nothing will ever come between you and your reverence and adoration for God. Yet it happened. Wrong desires have stepped in, and you have found yourself caught in a web. And you just don't know how to get out.

The people of Israel were caught in the web of sin; they were heavily involved in idolatry. God was displeased with them, so he instructed Moses, "You shall destroy their altars, and break down their sacred pillars, and cut down their wooden images, and burn their carved images with fire" (Deuteronomy 7:5 NKJV). God wasn't pleased that the people of Israel were serving other gods and walking in sinful ways. God wanted them to do something about their sins—to change their wrongdoings. Likewise, we need to break bad habits, shatter and cut down every wrong desire, and even burn and destroy things that come between our souls and God.

God is so much interested in our souls. Holiness is his deep heart cry.

Despite the Israelites' idolatrous and sinful ways, Moses

still told them, "You are a holy people to the Lord your God; the Lord your God has chosen you to be a people for Himself, a special treasure above all the peoples on the face of the earth" (Deuteronomy 7:6 NKJV). Wow! God didn't stop loving these people; he continued to love and show mercy to them. Because of his grace, he viewed them as holy people, his treasure, his chosen people.

God cared about the Israelites' heart condition. I'm glad God doesn't care for only one set of people; he cares about every individual on this earth despite our ethnicity, background, or credentials. In fact, God puts value on us. That's the reason Jesus died a painful and horrifying death on the cross. For us. Through Jesus's death, he freed mankind from the curse and enslavement of sin.

As believers in Christ, we now understand that sin should *not* have power over us, because God has given us a "new nature," which is the Holy Spirit living inside us. The Holy Spirit will fill us with a burning love for the things of God. It's a supernatural love. The Holy Spirit is God's abiding presence with us to enable us to overcome every sin, temptation, bad habits, and wrong desires—or anything that will come between our soul and God.

Do you feel you are enslaved to sin? When you are a slave to something or a person, that thing or person has a stronghold on you. As believers, because of the "new nature" deposited in us, we now have great power—the Holy Spirit living in us. Therefore, we make a firm decision to put to death every single sin that once controlled our lives. First John 5:4 (, emphasis added) reminds us that "every child of God defeats this evil world, and we *achieve this victory through our faith in Christ*." Now tell yourself, "I will win this battle."

My Commitment

Dear heavenly Father, I now have a great longing in my heart to please you. Because of this "new nature" God has deposited in me, I won't allow sin or any temptation to have a hold on my life. From now onward, I choose to listen to the Holy Spirit and be obedient to you. Amen.

85

Strength for the Battle

The Lord your God is with you, the *Mighty Warrior* who saves. He will take great delight in you; in his love he will no longer rebuke you, but will rejoice over you with singing.
—Zephaniah 3:17 (NIV, emphasis added)

Is there a battle in your life that came as a surprise? Maybe you just accomplished something and felt so proud about it that all you wanted to do was to celebrate. As seen in 2 Samuel 5, David had just been anointed king of Israel; instead of celebrating this victory, suddenly, he was attacked by his enemies, the Philistines (2 Samuel 5:17–18). The shocking news of the approaching army soon hit him, and he had no other option but to respond accordingly.

The Philistines were not pleased about hearing the news that David had been anointed king. They had already mobilized all their forces to capture him. This was a critical moment for David. He was uncertain about what to do since the Philistines had already spread out across the valley of Rephaim. I'm glad David didn't crumble in fear, but he sought the Lord for divine guidance.

The Lord loves when we come to him for help. He answered David by telling him, "Go ahead. I will certainly hand [the

Philistines] over to you" (2 Samuel 5:19). These were the words David needed to hear at that moment. He knew God kept his Word, so he obeyed the Lord, and with confidence, he went out and fought the Philistines.

That day David defeated his enemies. Note his response: "The Lord did it! He burst through my enemies like a raging flood!" (2 Samuel 5:20). David didn't take credit for the victory; he realized God was the one with him throughout the whole ordeal. David didn't fight the battle in his ability and the skills he had acquired; almighty God was the one who had helped him to win.

Afterward, David was so overwhelmed with joy that he named the place Baal-perazim, which means "the Lord who bursts through" (2 Samuel 5:20). In fierce battles, do you trust the Lord to "burst through"? Like David, we can put our confidence in God, knowing he won't fail us; he will "burst through" all those struggles and situations that look impossible, and give us the victory.

Proverbs 3:5 (NIV) states, "Trust in the Lord with all your heart; and lean not on your own understanding." When we trust the Lord, we are solely dependent on God, realizing he is sovereign. This means he has the last say in any given situation. David knew what it meant to trust God. That was the reason, David didn't lean on his own understanding; he had learned the secret of waiting on God to give him directions as to what to do. How do we wait on God when we are in a battle? We wait hopefully, knowing God is our help and shield (Psalm 33:20). God is the one who will see us through.

David was a human being just like any of us. He had the same tendencies to become fearful and lose faith. But when we look at David's life, there is a marked confidence he had in God. This is because he placed himself in a position to hear from God. He didn't allow other voices around him to nullify God's voice.

David trusted in God's supernatural ability to fight for him. He believed the Lord, the mighty Warrior, was with him in every battle he faced. God was the one who rescued him. Like David, let's wholly lean on God.

What is your response when faced with a battle? Do you allow fear to overtake you, or do you make a deliberate effort to listen to what God is saying to you about the situation? In Psalm 20:6–7 (NIV), David asserted, "Now this I know: The Lord gives victory to his anointed … Some trust in chariots and some in horses, but we trust in the name of the Lord our God." Trusting in God and not in human effort is important when we face fierce battles. Even now, talk to God in prayer.

Prayer

Lord, I choose to listen to and obey your voice. Reveal to me what I need to do in this battle. Although this battle looks so fierce and difficult to conquer, I believe you will strengthen me and give me the victory. Thank you for showing me the path I need to take. Amen!

Let Go of Anger

A soft answer turns away wrath, but
a harsh word stirs up anger.
—Proverbs 15:1 (NKJV)

One of the huge problems many people must deal with is the burden of a sin or weakness in their lives. This can come in many forms or shapes. For instance, anger is a huge problem many people are struggling with. If this is the case, we need to come to that place where we acknowledge that we have an anger issue. Some of the indicators are: being hot tempered, impatient, or full of rage; getting into conflicts and quarrels; and speaking filthy language (Proverbs 15:18; Colossians 3:8 NIV).

As human beings, we don't like to admit we can't control our emotions or temper. You might even be saying, "I want to do what is right, but I can't. I want to do what is good, but I don't. I don't want to do what is wrong, but I do it anyway" (Romans 7:18–19). Is this your heart cry? You want to do what is right and good, but somehow you are struggling to make this happen? That's because anger has the potential of enslaving us.

We must come to the place where we want to be set free from anger. Without a doubt, you are miserable. Plus, you aren't feeling confident about yourself. No one wants to feel this way. That's why this is *not* the time to give up but to come to terms with yourself. We need to ask, "Where is this anger stemming from? What am I so bitter about? Who has hurt me so badly that I can't forgive him or her?" Dealing with anger is our responsibility. It's a choice we need to make to resolve this problem.

We don't need to be stuck in this unhealthy habit of anger; we can overcome it. I believe God has wired each of us to take control of our situations in life and behavior. If we persist in this unruly behavior of losing our temper, we will always feel dissatisfied and frustrated with ourselves. Some people have even gone to professional counseling to help them sort out where the anger is coming from. That's a good choice. Maybe that anger stems from something that happened in the past that you have never really dealt with. Maybe it's generational, so it appears as a norm to you. So you continue in this lifestyle. You realize that even a little situation can make you snap. If this is the case, then it's time to confront the root cause of this anger; this is a good place to start.

God wants to show us his mercy. This means he will pour out his love and grace on us to help us conquer this anger problem; it doesn't have to hold onto us. Even now, ask God to give you wisdom and understanding as to how to overcome it. Thankfully, this problem of anger has a solution.

The beautiful thing about God is that he isn't mad with us because we are angry, especially if someone has deliberately hurt us. However, God doesn't want us to stay being angry for an entire lifetime. He wants us to approach him. Let's be honest and cry out to God, knowing that the answer to this problem of anger lies in Jesus Christ. According Galatians 5:23 (NIV), "The fruit of the Holy Spirit is … Self-Control." As we depend on the Holy Spirit, he will give us the know-how to control that anger issue and overcome it. This is when the healing process starts.

Is God opening your heart to work on this anger issue? What are some strategies you plan to use to overcome this problem? At this point, remember, you aren't alone. As you talk with your counselor or a friend you can trust, be honest and open to suggestions as to how to deal with this problem. Most of all, talk to God. Hide in God. His everlasting arms will steady you and make you strong (Deuteronomy 33:27). Also, examine the activities you are presently involved in. Then, break off from any activity that is triggering this anger and get involved in constructive activities that will bring you fulfillment and peace of mind. Even now, as God gives you wisdom and understanding, declare the following:

Declaration

Thank you, God, that you are working in me. I know you will not leave me as a victim to anger, but you will provide me with the power and ability to do what pleases you. With your strength and my decision to work on this persistent problem, I believe I will overcome anger. Anger will *not* control me.

Weeping to Singing

Every day I will praise you and extol your name for
ever and ever. Great is the Lord and most worthy
of praise; his greatness no one can fathom.
—Psalm 145:2–3 (NIV)

I'm glad the psalmist embraced this truth that the Lord is most
worthy of praise. In Revelation 5, John in a vision saw and
heard an angel shouting, "Who is worthy to open the scroll
and to loose its seals? And no one in heaven or on the earth
or under the earth was able to open the scroll, or to look at
it" ((Revelation 5:2–3 NKJV). As a result, John wept bitterly.
The beauty about this situation is that John foresaw the plight
humanity would have been in if no one was found worthy.

Clearly, he envisioned that mankind would be lost without a
Savior. He saw that we would be stuck in our sins, wrongdoings,
and bondage. The devil would have loved for this to happen to
us. I can imagine Satan's mocking grin because there is no way
of escape for us. Thank goodness, Jesus's death on the cross
changed the whole scenario. Can you picture how much Jesus
suffered for us? Hanging there on the cross—blood streaming
down his body and the nails piercing his hands and feet? What

excruciating pain he went through just to rescue us from sin. Jesus did this because of his great love for us.

In John's vision, one of the twenty-four elders told him to stop weeping because the Lion of the tribe of Judah had already won the victory (Revelation 5:4). He is the one worthy to open the scroll. This profound truth gives us hope. When no one else was found worthy, Jesus, referred to as the Lion of the tribe of Judah was. Jesus is the only One willing to be slaughtered on the cross; his blood has delivered and liberated people from all nations and tribes from their flaws, bondage, and sins (Revelation 5:9). That's the beauty of Jesus's love. On the cross, he died personally for you. He died to liberate all of us from the entrapment of the works of darkness.

What happened when Jesus died on the cross can be described as, "It is finished" (John 19:30 NKJV). That was Jesus's last cry, symbolizing that he had completed his assignment on earth, which his Father had designated to him. Yes, his huge sacrifice of dying on the cross for our sins made a way for us to be forgiven for every single sin. This means we don't need to be carrying around the burden of sin anymore. In fact, "when [Jesus] was hung on the cross, he took upon himself the curse for our wrongdoing" (Galatians 3:13). Because of Jesus's obedience, he has won the victory for all of us. No one is excluded.

Jesus will never leave us in Satan's grip. The Lord, our mighty Warrior, will fight for us; he will snatch us away from Satan's trap because we are his beloved children. He will no longer rebuke you, but he will rejoice over you with singing (Zephaniah 3:17). Isn't it beautiful to know that our lives don't need to be filled with weeping and sorrow? Jesus's death on the cross has made it possible for us to have a song in our hearts— laughter instead of mourning, victory instead of defeat.

This vision John saw is so authentic that it made me reflect on my past life. There was a time when I felt so unworthy that I thought God wouldn't accept me. I'm glad that I now understand that Jesus's death on the cross makes me worthy of his love. On the cross, he forgave mankind of every single sin and weakness. He carried them so I don't need to be burdened with them all through life. Actually, God wants to personally deposit something precious and beautiful in our lives that will satisfy the very core of our souls. That's the reason we need to continuously come to the cross and surrender our lives to him.

Do you believe the blood of Jesus can deliver you from any sin or weakness? The blood of Jesus brings us into freedom. By faith, as you surrender your life to Jesus, he will cleanse and forgive you of all your sins, and he will change your heart. Now you will become more conscious of God, and you will want to please him. Then he will fill you with a *new joy* and excitement. Remember, we now belong to Jesus; we are conquerors over every sin, weakness, or addiction. Even now let's say this prayer:

Prayer

Jesus, thank you for dying on the cross for me. Because of this great sacrifice you made, I'm not a captive of sin any longer. God in his great love for me has canceled any record of those sins I committed. Now I am set free from the bondage of sin. My new song is "The Curse of Wrongdoings Has Been Broken in My Life." Amen.

88

The Obstacles Must Come Down

Thanks be to God, who gives us the victory
through our Lord Jesus Christ.
—1 Corinthians 15:57 (NKJV)

Are you in a battle where you feel you need the Lord's help and guidance to conquer something that seems gigantic or impossible? Are there hindrances or barriers in your path preventing you from seeing your victory? In Joshua 6, Joshua and the Israelites encountered a huge obstacle, the walls of Jericho. From a human standpoint, those walls must have seemed impenetrable or even impossible for them to conquer. But Joshua knew he needed to press through and do the task God had commanded him to do.

When we encounter difficulties, what is our response? God had given Joshua this instruction: "You shall march around the city, all you men of war; you shall go all around the city once. This you shall do six days. And seven priests shall bear seven trumpets of rams' horns before the ark. But the seventh day you shall march around the city seven times, and the priests shall blow the trumpets" (Joshua 6:3–4 NKJV). To human eyes, this plan might not have looked like a war strategy. The cry of the doubter will be "How could strong, huge walls collapse because of people marching around them!" However, a person of faith sees differently. He or she sees there are no limitations with God. All things are possible.

When God gives us an instruction, we need to follow through with it, even though it may not make any sense to us. That's when we need to act in faith, not by our own intuition. In this battle, God gave Joshua, the leader of the Israelites, a detailed and precise strategy, reassuring him that he would conquer Jericho, its king, and all its strong warriors. Joshua fully well knew he was going into this battle with all of heaven backing him.

What's so beautiful about this scene is that the people blew the ram's horns and marched in the presence of the Lord. The ark of the Lord's covenant followed them. Yes, the presence of God is the most important weapon we can carry in a battle, coupled with obedience.

Although the gigantic walls stood as a huge barrier, the people were willing to do whatever God had commanded them to do. They were confident about each step they took. Their continual marching, blowing of the horns, and walking in silence, carrying the presence of God, attested to the fact that they believed God's Word. They anticipated seeing the promise fulfilled.

On the seventh day, God made an even greater demand on the people. He instructed them to march around the town seven times. When God makes a greater demand on us, what is our response? The Israelites were submissive to God's command, and God didn't fail them. At *the end of their obedience,* just like God had promised them, the walls of Jericho "fell down flat!" (Joshua 6:20 NKJV).

Note: the people had one mind and purpose. They unified as a people, keeping their eyes on the goal. The Israelites didn't have their own agendas or plans. They had to follow all the instructions of Joshua with precision. Rebelling or turning aside to do their own thing couldn't have been on their minds. Even if this was the case, I'm sure they would have had to deal with it accordingly so God's plan could be accomplished.

Following God's path and plan will always entail that we look "unto Jesus, the author and finisher of our faith" (Hebrews 12:2 NKJV). God being our focus is key to achieving the goals and dreams God has placed in our hearts. Obeying, mixed with praise, and keeping our eyes on God and not on obstacles will always bring about the victory.

Are you looking forward to seeing God breakthrough in a particular area of your life? The Israelites' secret in winning this great victory was their submissive attitude and choosing *not* to keep their eyes on the obstacles but to look to God. Also, their obedience stood out. We need to keep on doing whatever God is asking us to do until we see the victory. Even now, we need to settle in our minds that we will listen to the voice of the Lord. God's thoughts are far higher than ours, and his ways are far beyond our imaginations. He is the one who will perform the miracle. Let's keep believing.

Declaration

I choose to be in your presence. In faith, I'm going to start shouting and praising your name, because you are with me in this situation. I believe all the *walls preventing me from seeing my breakthrough* will collapse because I serve a powerful God who won't fail me. You are the mighty Warrior, who will help me win this battle.

89

Say No to Temptation

In Luke 4, we see Jesus had been fasting for forty days, so he was extremely hungry. In that moment of physical weakness, the devil sneaked up to Jesus and tried to trap him so he could fall into temptation. Does this sound familiar? How many times have we fallen into temptations because we haven't been watchful? The devil knows the exact time when he should target us. In the case of Jesus, he had already committed to his heavenly Father to obey him. He was bent on doing his Father's will and to overcome the temptations Satan threw at him.

In this conversion below between Jesus and the devil, let's see how Jesus overcame the devil (Luke 4:3–12).

Devil: "If you are the Son of God, tell this stone to become a loaf of bread."

Jesus: "No! The Scriptures say, 'People do not live by bread alone.'"

Devil: "I will give you the glory of these kingdoms and authority over them, because they are mine to give to anyone I please. I will give it all to you if you worship me."

Jesus: "The Scriptures say, 'You must worship the Lord your God and serve only him.'"

Satan: "If you are the Son of God, jump off! For the Scriptures say, 'He will order his angels to protect and guard you. And they will hold you up with their hands so you won't even hurt your foot on a stone.'"

Jesus: "The Scriptures also say, 'You must not test the Lord your God.'"

Notice that all three times the devil tried to tempt Jesus, Jesus used the Word to overcome him. How much more do we need to use the Word to overcome the schemes and power of the devil? In vulnerable moments, the devil might try to tempt us or lie to us by filling our minds with wrong thoughts and ideas; these are all strategies he uses to distract us from following God with all our hearts.

Let's not be victims of the adversary's plans. Like Jesus, let's use the Word of God to counteract all the schemes the devil fabricates to use against us. What are some lies Satan tells God's people? One huge lie we frequently tell ourselves is this: "There is no way that you can overcome this sin. You have been meddling in it too long. It will always overtake you. Just stop trying. You're only frustrating yourself." This is a huge lie from Satan to trick God's people to continue in the practice of sin.

Note: since the beginning of time, the devil has been

devising all kinds of tactics to get God's people to sin. We see this in the garden of Eden when he tempted Eve and Adam. Satan perfectly well knows that sin is a bondage. We were born into sin. There is no way mankind can free themselves from sin. It's like glue on us. That's because our sinful nature weren't yet cut away. But when we receive Jesus into our lives, God makes us alive in Christ, and he forgives all our sins. In fact, he canceled the record of all the sins the devil has been accusing us of by nailing them to the cross (Colossians 2:13–14). Isn't this mind blowing?

God canceled *all* our sins.

I'm glad Jesus wants to deliver us from the bondage of sin. Like Jesus we need to use the Word of God to overcome all Satan's strategies to get us to sin.

As children of God, we can't afford to be negligent and careless about our walk with the Lord, because sin will always be lurking in the dark. That's the reason we always need to be conscious of the devil's schemes and watchful. With God's help and anointing, we have the power to free ourselves from falling into temptation and sin.

How do we actually overcome the strategies of the devil? Without the blood of Jesus, we cannot be delivered from our sins and weaknesses. But being cleansed or being set free from sin doesn't happen magically. It's a faith walk! We cannot conquer the works of darkness by our human effort. Because of Jesus's death on the cross, the power of sin has been broken. And God draws us to accept Jesus's love. As we surrender our wills to our Father, God provides the grace and strength through the Holy Spirit to overcome every single temptation or sin we would ever have to face from day to day.

Commitment

Lord, I commit myself to reading your Word and to use it to defeat all the temptations that come my way. Thank you for equipping me with the *Holy Spirit, who is working in me*, so my desire has changed. Through you, I *now* have the power to overcome sin and carnal desires.

90

A Specific Strategy for the Battle

When you are afraid of what the outcome might be, what is your response? In a battle, do you depend solely on God or look for a strong and courageous person to help you? Like all of us, we want to win. But certain battles can be won only by using wise stratagems and listening to specific instructions.

In the Old Testament days, the psalmist David fought many battles and won victory after victory. What was David's secret or strategy for winning so many battles? First, David was anointed by God. The Lord God of heaven's armies was with him. For that reason, he became more and more powerful.

Yet in each battle David faced, he solely depended on God to give him directions.

In 2 Samuel 5, when the Philistines planned to attack David, again he went before God to ask him for guidance. Note: David had already conquered the Philistines at the same place, the valley of Rephaim. So he could have easily decided he was quite capable of defeating them again (2 Samuel 5:17–20 NIV). But David realized he needed to rely on God for every battle.

In another battle recorded in 2 Samuel 5:22–25 (NIV), God gave David a specific strategy. God told David to listen for a sound like marching in the tops of the poplar trees, which would be the signal for him to strike down the Philistines. In this case, the Lord was requiring David to be in a certain place (by the poplar trees) to listen for a particular sound (marching feet at the treetops) and to have an attitude of being alert and ready to take action.

What's more, God's instruction to David was, "Do not go straight up, but circle around behind them and attack them in front of the poplar trees" (2 Samuel 5:23 NIV). Although David may not have understood why he needed to follow all those instructions, he knew one thing—God is an *all-knowing God.* He knows all the circumstances and plans surrounding this battle, so he would know exactly what David should do to win this battle.

Sometimes God's commands might seem bizarre to human ears, but they are always important steps for us to follow. David knew that the key to winning this battle lay in strategically obeying each instruction the Lord had given him. For that reason, the Lord honored him by helping him to win another great victory. Yes, God honors obedience.

David had come to a place in God where he could praise God even before the battle was won and also amid the battle. In Psalm 144:1–2, he proclaimed. "Praise the Lord, who is my rock. He trains my hands for war and gives my fingers skill for battle. He is my loving ally and my fortress, my tower of safety, my rescuer. He is my shield, and *I take refuge in him*" (emphasis added). David learned the secret of taking refuge in his God, so when the battle seemed to be raging, God comforted, strengthened, and calmed his emotions, and showed him the path to take.

If you are losing one battle after another, don't give up. Wait on God for directions. Clearly, God doesn't want us to falter. He wants us to look closely at our lives and see what adjustments we need to make so we can win. God has equipped us with the Holy Spirit to be winners; he will help and guide you to use wisdom to turn away from the wrong and evil paths. In fact, he will show and teach you the way to be victorious.

Is there a battle in your life that is scaring you? Or are you believing God to give you a strategy as to how to win it? Many times, we may not understand why the battle we're in seems to be raging, or it feels endless. But God loves when we can trust him. Like David, let's be alert to hear God's instructions. This is the time for us to wait on God to give us a strategy as to how to handle our emotions, the path we need to take, the kind of prayers we need to pray, and what portions of the Word we need to read. Even now, tell God the following:

Prayer

Lord, although I don't understand why I am facing this battle, I choose to trust you. Give me clear directions as to the path you want me to take, and I will be obedient. Even now I declare that my soul will find rest in you despite my circumstances.

The Winner in You

All of us have some sort of a giant in our path we need to deal with. Whether it's a sickness, a disappointment, an area of weakness, a temptation, a painful experience, a negative emotion, people's criticism, or even a lack of willpower and courage, we definitely want to overcome it. No one wants to stay defeated. Therefore, this is the perfect time to remind yourselves that there's something inside us that cannot be extinguished. That something is a greater power living inside us, strengthening, comforting, and empowering us. That power is what gives us the ability to win. Through the upcoming chapters in "The Winner in You," you will find out how both men and women overcame the Goliaths in their lives. They realized the giants were there for them to conquer. For that reason, some of the characters chose to sing and praise their way through each stumbling block they encountered. And God didn't fail them. As always, he stepped in and showed them his amazing and extraordinary strength amid dark circumstances and raging battles.

91

Conquer the Giants in Your Path

How would you have felt if your brothers tried to push you away from the very thing you really wanted to be a part of? In the Bible story of David and Goliath, David's brothers tried to prevent him from fighting Goliath. David had to ignore his brothers' remarks and even the king's, and do what he believed God had appointed him to do. He didn't allow opposition and people's views to stop him from carrying out what God had placed in his heart. This was a pivotal moment in David's life; he couldn't allow this moment to pass him by. Pivotal moments are planned by God, so let's never take them lightly.

In 1 Samuel 17, we see a battle between the Philistines and the Israelites. David's brothers were fighting in Saul's army on the side of Israel. So David's father sent him to the camp to take food to his brothers (1 Samuel 17:17). Little did David realize this was a trip God himself had orchestrated. He thought he was just bringing food for his brothers, but God had a greater plan in mind.

When David arrived at the camp, he was surprised to hear Goliath, the Philistine champion, taunting and threatening the army of Israel. The Israelites were so afraid of Goliath that as soon as they saw him, they started running away (1 Samuel

17:24). These people saw Goliath as a huge giant, whom they couldn't defeat. Are there some giants or obstacles in your life that seem so huge that, instead of confronting them, you find yourself running from them?

Let's see how David dealt with his giant.

In David's mind, Goliath was defying the armies of his God. David saw Goliath as his enemy, who deserved to die, and you can sense the 'warrior spirit' rising up in him. At that moment, David might not have even realized what God was doing—he would be the instrument God was about to use to defeat this big giant. However, his brothers saw him as a meddler.

David's oldest brother belittled him, saying, "Why did you come down here? And with whom have you left those few sheep in the wilderness? I know your pride and the insolence of your heart, for you have come down to see the battle" (1 Samuel 17:28 NKJV). David's brothers associated him with being in the background, taking care of sheep, while they should be in the forefront. They looked at him negatively—as being full of pride. These men had limited vision; they couldn't see that God had a special purpose for David being there at that specific moment.

Even King Saul saw David as being incapable of fighting this battle. When he told the king he wanted to fight Goliath, he thought it was a ridiculous idea. He saw him as only a boy compared to Goliath, whom he viewed as a man of war since his youth (1 Samuel 17: 33).

This was a moment when no one believed in David. Thank goodness David saw himself in a different light. When everyone else is viewing you negatively, how do you view yourself? In moments like these, what are you believing and confessing? I love David's affirmation. He said to Saul, "Your servant used to keep his father's sheep, and when a lion or a bear came and took a lamb out of the flock, I went out after it and struck it, and delivered the lamb from its mouth ... Your servant has killed both lion and bear ... The Lord, who delivered me from the paw of the lion and from the paw of the bear, He will deliver me from the hand of this Philistine" (1 Samuel 17:34–37 NKJV). David knew that when he killed both the lion and the bear, he did it with the Lord's anointing on his life. In his frail human strength, he would never have been able to accomplish this.

When Goliath realized David would be his opponent in the battle, he started to intimidate him by telling him he would give his flesh to the birds and wild animals (1 Samuel 17:44). I can picture his tone; this was Goliath's strategy of driving fear in David. As always, the enemy will try to weaken our faith by using fear. But with confidence, David told Goliath, "You come to me with a sword, with a spear, and with a javelin. But I come to you in the name of the Lord of hosts, the God of the armies of Israel, whom you have defied. This day the Lord will deliver you into my hand" (1 Samuel 17:45–46 NKJV). David knew winning this battle lay in the fact that God was invincible in battle. Because God was on David's side, he effortlessly triumphed over the Philistine with only a sling and a stone (1 Samuel 17:49).

The Lord anointed David for this specific task. For every battle or assignment in our path, God has promised to anoint us with strength, ability, and power to overcome and win.

No one in his or her wildest dream believed that David, a mere youth, would have been able to fight a big giant like Goliath and conquer him. *The giants in our lives are there for us to defeat.* God will give us strategies and show us step by step how to deal with the giants we face. As he does, with the help of the Holy Spirit, let's overcome what we are destined to conquer.

Think for a moment. What are some strategies God has given to you to win the battle you are now facing? As you spend some time in prayer, God will show you what to do. In the text, even the king doubted David's ability to win. People's views and even our own view of ourselves will drive fear and doubt in our spirits. But we must see ourselves as winners and conquerors. We need to see "the Lord, [as being] strong and mighty; the Lord [is] invincible in battle" (Psalm 24:8). Therefore, with God on our side, we cannot lose. We will win every battle that comes our way. Let us declare the following:

Declaration

I see myself winning and conquering all the strategies the enemy has devised to make me fall. The Lord who rescued David will also rescue me; therefore I am anointed with power from on high to win this battle. You will rescue me from the claws of any evil force. From today onward, I choose to keep my eyes on you.

92

Let My Soul Sing

One night as I was listening to the song "How Great Thou Art," the Lord ministered to me through these words:

> Then sings my soul,
> My Saviour God, to Thee,
> How great Thou art,
> How great Thou art!

Our souls can actually sing. They can be filled with gladness. But so many times, our souls are sad because of unpleasant circumstances around us, puzzling situations, unanswered questions, or struggles deep inside, so the singing stops. But Psalm 42:11 (NIV) tells us we need to command our souls to sing by saying, "Why, my soul, are you downcast? Why so disturbed within me? Put your hope in God, for I will yet praise him, my Savior and my God." Yes, there will always be challenges, setbacks, and obstacles in our paths that can cause us to become disturbed and downcast. However, when we choose to praise God, the very core of our hearts is responding to God, the Savior of our souls—our God, who will not forsake us but deliver us.

In Luke 1, we see Mary was faced with an unexpected and

puzzling situation. Although she might not have understood how she, a virgin, could bear a son conceived by the Holy Spirit, she responded, "Oh, how my soul praises the Lord. How my spirit rejoices in God my Savior! For he took notice of his lowly servant girl" (Luke 1:46–48).

Wow! What a revelation! During that time, Mary must have been labeled as deceitful, unfaithful, insincere, and dishonest for being pregnant, but she still praised God. She acknowledged that God had taken notice of her as "his lowly servant girl." Mary was truly humble and submissive to God's will. It is no wonder that God handpicked her from among all the women from every generation and nation to carry the Messiah in her body. God had prepared her for that particular time and specific purpose. Mary considered it a privilege, so she gladly honored and praised God.

Like Mary, we might not understand everything about the circumstances we find ourselves in, but we need to know God will deliver our souls from anything too overwhelming. God is interested in our souls; that's why how we respond to him is so important. If there are challenges and puzzling situations in our lives, instead of bowing our heads in shame and defeat, we can command our souls to sing, "My Savior God to me. How great thou art." Jesus, our Savior, who is great and full of kindness and love, will deliver us so our souls can indeed sing for joy.

Many times, we must choose either to sing or to have a pity party. God commands us to sing praises to him (Psalm 47:6–7). Singing not only changes our demeanor, but God is pleased when we sing to him. Amid the toughest times, we can choose to praise God instead of complaining or grumbling about our circumstances. When we look at Mary's life, we see she was rejoicing in God; she didn't blame him for putting her in such uncomfortable conditions. Nor did she refuse to accept this responsibility.

Despite the many questions that must have gone through Mary's mind, she still extolled God. Clearly, she chose to trust in God; she believed he was faithful and true to his Word. Like Mary, why not choose to praise God by telling him, "I will sing of the Lord's great love forever; with my mouth I will make your faithfulness known through all generations. I will declare that your love stands firm forever" (Psalm 89:1–2 NIV)?

Have you ever found yourself in a puzzling situation that made absolutely no sense to you? Has that situation changed your perception of God or his Word? Even though this situation may seem perplexing to you, do you think God has a plan for your life, like he had for Mary? How do you see God? As great and mighty or as weak and uncaring? The fact is, God's love is steadfast and unfailing. He sees the many conflicts in your mind with eyes of compassion. Even now, as you start to acknowledge God as your great Deliverer, who knows exactly what is going on deep inside you, he is able to fix what seems wrong. Why not start praising God for doing that great work in your life?

Prayer

Lord, please forgive me for not praising you as I should. I realize my soul can sing. When tough circumstances make me waver, like Mary, I will trust you. Because of your faithfulness, I will sing instead of pouting and moping. I refuse to stay in defeat and sadness. I acknowledge that you are my Savior, so you will deliver my soul. Today I give you a high note of praise for all the victories ahead.

93

Jesus Is Moved by a Woman's Faith

Have you ever seen someone suffering because of a sickness? This is a painful experience to watch, especially if it's someone you love. This can really break your heart. The woman in Luke 8 had been suffering from a blood condition for twelve years. But what is even worse is that this woman "had spent all her livelihood on physicians and could not be healed by any" (Luke 8:43 NKJV). As we can see, this woman was financially and emotionally broken.

You can feel this woman's anguish. But what is so beautiful about her is her fight for survival—her determination to receive her healing. I believe when she heard about Jesus performing many miracles by healing all kinds of diseases and sicknesses, and casting out demons, something happened deep in her spirit. A new courage and faith rose within her. Yes, she was quite aware that women were supposed to be in the background. And if they had a bleeding condition like she did, she wasn't supposed to be seen in public places. But this woman was determined to change the status quo; she couldn't allow people's expectations to keep her from a miracle. She had to find Jesus. She had to get that one touch from him.

I can picture this woman getting so excited that she refused to stay in her house any longer. With new hope rising within her, she made the first step; in faith she left her house. Note her tenacity: somehow she knew where Jesus was ministering, and she found her way there. She was so bent on getting her miracle that she ignored traditional customs and pressed her way through the crowds until she was standing close to Jesus. At that moment, Jesus realized someone had deliberately touched him in faith, for he felt healing power go out from him. This woman's deliberate effort to personally touch Jesus stands out. That's because she firmly believed Jesus would heal her. Realizing it was a touch of faith, Jesus said to her, "Daughter, be of good cheer; your faith has made you well. Go in peace" (Luke 8:48 NKJV). What a miracle! What an expression of faith!

The woman with the blood condition teaches us a beautiful lesson about faith. Let's look at what she did.

- She must have *heard* about Jesus's healing power, and her faith became active.
- She took the *risk* of leaving her home to find Jesus, even though she knew she wasn't supposed to be seen in public places because of her bleeding problem.
- She captures the *truth* that Jesus's power is real.
- This woman's very *thoughts* embody faith.
- From thinking she would receive her healing, she *envisioned* leaving that place healed. There, she said to herself: "If I can just touch his robe, I will be healed" (Matthew 9:21). This woman had already rehearsed the whole scene in her mind, and standing in front of Jesus, she saw her miracle come to reality.
- She didn't doubt, but she *edged* her way through the crowd, confident that she would receive her healing.

- She *stepped out* in faith and deliberately touched the hem of Jesus's garment.
- Because of this woman's persistent and *unwavering* faith in Jesus, she received her miracle.
- *This woman had a fight in her* that said no to unbelief and fear—and yes to divine healing.
- She had this kind of faith: "if you have faith and don't doubt … You can even say to this mountain, 'May you be lifted up and thrown into the sea,' and *it will happen.* You can pray for anything, and if you have faith, you will receive it" (Matthew 21:21–22 (emphasis added).

Like this woman, what are your thoughts like? Are you seeing that just one touch of Jesus will bring about the miracle you are anticipating? In Luke 17:5–6, Jesus told his disciples, "If you had faith even as small as a mustard seed, you could say to this mulberry tree, 'May you be uprooted and be planted in the sea,' and it would obey you!" The mustard seed, though small, is planted in the ground, which grows into a tall tree. In the same way, our little faith can grow as we keep watering it through our praying, reading the Word, listening to the voice of God, and being obedient. Then, like this woman with the blood issue, we too can operate in faith and see our miracles come to pass. Even now, let's pray.

Prayer

Lord, like this woman, I believe your power is real. So I come in faith, believing I will receive my miracle. I push back fear and doubt, and I now look forward to receive my healing. Amen.

94

Overcome Areas of Defeat

Let us strip off every weight that slows us down, especially the sin that so easily trips us up. And let us run with endurance the race God has set before us. We do this by keeping our eyes on Jesus, the champion who initiates and perfects our faith.

—Hebrews 12:1–2

Is there an area in your life or a situation in your past that constantly makes you feel inadequate, weak, or hopeless? If there is, don't be discouraged. Every one of us has to deal with some form of weakness or negative emotion in our lives. Although we might not be living in sin per se, there are definitely areas in our lives—things we don't feel good about, things that can weigh us down—we need to conquer.

One particular subject I think every person should deal with is *the past*. One thing we know about past mistakes is that the devil brings them up over and over again, and like a big whip, he spanks us with it. Spanking hurts! That's the devil's intention—to hurt and condemn us for our past sins or even for feeling vulnerable. We need to know that the devil's top priority is to destroy us (John 10:10). He will try to do everything he can to make us feel horrible about ourselves; if he can succeed in doing this, he will accomplish what he set out to do.

What are some of the lies the devil tells us about the past? I can relate to this. There was a period when I felt so unworthy, guilty, and condemned because I had walked away from the Lord that I had a difficult time forgiving myself. I felt that I had failed the Lord. For that reason, I called all kinds of prayer lines to find out what I should do; for a while it seemed like nothing helped. Satan just bombarded my mind, telling me I had missed the mark and that God would never use me again.

What horror!

While the devil wants to corrupt our minds with wrong and negative thoughts, God wants us to think positively about ourselves. Satan isn't our friend; he is ruthless in his pursuit to make us feel defeated and powerless. For that reason, he constantly uses all kinds of strategies to convince us that we will never win the battle. His plan is to keep us from moving forward; he wants us to give up. In other words, he has been lying to us all the time. The truth is, the devil will always be scared of these two things: when we turn the pages of the Word of God and discover we are more than conquerors (Romans 8:37); and when we get on our knees and approach a merciful and holy God, who will transform our hearts and teach us to walk in holiness.

Note: God's greatest joy is for us to enjoy life by taking our eyes off past weaknesses and mistakes, and fixing our eyes on him. However, too many times our eyes are so fixated on the flaws in our lives that they block us from seeing God and his good plans for our lives. Like the apostle Paul, we need to make a conscious effort to forget the past by throwing off our former way of life. Instead, we should let the Holy Spirit renew our thoughts and attitudes. As we put on our new nature, which God has deposited in us, we will truly be righteous and holy like God (Ephesians 4:23–24). With this new mindset, I believe we will conquer all the negativity lurking in our minds, and we will press onward to do all God has called us to do.

God desires us to live life to the fullest. Yes, there will always be struggles we will need to deal with from time to time. Thank goodness God has promised to walk with us through those tough times. God doesn't want to see us defeated and wallowing in our past failures and present doubts. That's why he has already made provision for us to live a victorious life. In fact, God assures us, "My grace is sufficient for you, for My strength is made perfect in weakness" (2 Corinthians 12:9 NKJV). In actuality, God is saying to us that his supernatural strength is made available to us in those weak areas of our lives. He is the one perfecting us so we can walk in his ways.

Do you believe that through Christ we can have a right relationship with God? Yes, we now have a chance to *experience a new life in Christ*; we are now equipped with new strength and victory over the past. Tell God, "I break free from every area of defeat in my life; and I make this decision to press forward, keeping my eyes on you. Because you have purchased my freedom from every bondage and sin, I am no longer chained to my past failures." I now declare the following:

Declaration

Lord, I thank you that I am no longer condemned by myself, the devil, or others, because I am in Christ Jesus. From now onward, I choose *not* to walk according to the flesh or unholy desires but according to what the Holy Spirit wants me to do. I refuse to stay defeated, because through you I am more than a conqueror.

95

Sing Till the Answer Comes

> Don't let your heart be troubled
> Hold your head up high
> Don't fear no evil.
> —Hillsong United "Good Grace"

How do you react when an enemy tries to harm you? Depending on the extremity of the attack, everyone will respond differently. Some might fight back, throw their hands up in dismay, or even get military help; while those who know to trust in God will silently wait on God to rescue them.

Do you sometimes feel like you need to be protected from your enemies? In Psalm 59, the psalmist David cried out to the God of heaven's armies to rescue him from fierce enemies, because Saul had sent soldiers to watch his house to kill him. Can you imagine the stress David had to deal with during that time? Thankfully, David understood that all of heaven was on his side. He knew God would stand with him. He would help David triumph over his enemies (Psalm 59:3–5, 10).

Despite the circumstances, the psalmist continued to praise God by saying, "I will sing about your power. *Each morning I will sing with joy about your unfailing love*" (Psalm 59:16, emphasis added). Note his confidence in God; he was singing about God's power in the middle of a threatening situation. He wasn't giving in to fear and doubt. What's David's secret? David practiced spending time with God "each morning," so he was acquainted with God's ways. He understood that God's love was unfailing. Therefore God would fight for him.

Even when the battle is raging and our emotions are going wild, we shouldn't stop singing. Playing some good praise music is a good place to start, because singing praises to God paves the way for God to answer our prayers.

One song I particularly love to listen to is "Good Grace" by Hillsong United. During a down moment, as I was listening to this song, some of the words that really uplifted my spirit were "Don't let your heart be troubled, Hold your head up high. Don't fear no evil. Fix your eyes on this one truth; God is madly in love with you." Wow! What powerful lyrics! The songwriter reassures us of God's great love for us. In a fierce battle, sometimes all we need to know is that God is madly in love with us. This truth will calm our fears; instead of visualizing evil, we will see a loving God who won't allow the evil forces coming at us to overwhelm us.

God has the final word in every situation, not our enemy. This new mindset will change our attitude about our circumstances. Instead of hanging our head or crouching in fear, let's lift our heads up high, fixing our eyes on God, who has promised to keep us in perfect peace. Yes, God wants us to trust him, because in him is everlasting strength (Isaiah 26:3–4).

Trusting God amid a battle is an important part of winning the victory. The realization that God is our everlasting strength will ignite our faith to believe he will not let us fall. But he will keep us in perfect peace and give us the strength and courage we need for that particular battle.

I believe David learned that lesson. Even when his enemies

were seeking to kill him, he declared, "O my Strength, to you I sing praises, for you, O God, are my refuge, the God who shows me unfailing love" (Psalm 59:17). Singing was a huge part of David's life. For that reason, David sang with the understanding that the Lord would take care of his people; God was his refuge. He could rely on him to see him through.

When faced with stressful circumstances, how do you cope? Do you shut down because of fear and worry, or do you praise God? The song says, "Hold your head up high. Don't fear no evil." In the middle of this bad situation, David chose to sing praises to God; he knew his God was a mighty God, who would deliver him. And God didn't fail David; he kept his Word and rescued him from his enemies. Therefore, when we are in the middle of a battle, let's sing our way through until we see our victory. Make this a praise moment and tell God the following:

Praise Moment

Lord, although I'm feeling tense, fearful, and uncomfortable because of this situation, I choose to be like David. I will sing in the middle of this chaos. Because you are so madly in love with me, I know you will fight for me. So now I fear *no* evil, but I trust you for the victory ahead.

96

It's Not Over: Sin Is Defeated

Once I was broken,
But You loved my whole heart through.
Sin has no hold on me,
'Cause Your grace holds me now
—Hillsong United, "Whole Heart"

How do you view your life at this moment? Do you feel that it's so messed up or broken that there is no more hope for God to intervene? Despite people's negative views of themselves, God will always pursue their hearts. He's on the lookout to transform us so we can follow the plan he has for our lives. Even if you find yourselves chained to strongholds, bondage, pornography, past failures, and sins, God won't cast you away or stop chasing after you. In fact, this is the perfect time for God to do his most beautiful work. He longs for us to come to that place where sin doesn't have a hold on us because the grace of God has transformed our lives.

We see that sin and unrighteousness were prevailing among the people of Israel. The prophet Isaiah addressed this problem by saying, "What sorrow for those who drag their sins behind them with ropes made of lies" (Isaiah 5:18). Indeed, God doesn't want sin to hold on to us so strongly that we can't let go of it.

However, even amid sin, God's voice will always sound the loudest. It is the most powerful.

In the next chapter, the writer acknowledged, "It's all over! I am doomed, for I am a sinful man. I have filthy lips, and I live among a people with filthy lips" (Isaiah 6:5). Being caught in sin can make us feel like it's over, but because of God's unfailing love toward his people, he will still manifest himself to us. It is no wonder, despite his sins, Isaiah still had a vision of the Lord of heaven's armies. His vision of God makes us know how much God is interested in our souls. For that reason, one of the seraphim touched his lips and said, "See, this coal has touched your lips. Now your guilt is removed, and your sins are forgiven" (Isaiah 6:7). Wow! What an intervention from heaven! This shows that God is merciful and gracious, and he is more than able to penetrate deep into our hearts. He doesn't want us to stay in our sins but to deliver us from them.

Therefore, if you find yourself caught in the web of unholy living, don't think it's over. God's grace is still available to you; he will not write you off.

God has promised that his grace is sufficient for us; his strength is made perfect in those weak areas in our lives (2 Corinthians 12:9). This means God will supernaturally strengthen us by supplying us with his power to enable us to break the chains of sin and darkness. Then our whole lives will take a different turn, and we will say, like the songwriter, "Your Grace holds me now!"

Isaiah 53:3–5 conveys the beautiful work that Jesus did on the cross. Jesus chose to be crushed, beaten, pierced, and to be weighed down, because of our weaknesses, sorrows, and rebellion so we could be healed. The cross speaks of the great sacrifice Jesus made for us—all because he wants to deliver us from all our sins and rebellion. That's God showing us his grace.

You cannot think of grace without thinking of love, mercy, forgiveness, and—most of all—God's unfailing love. Grace is God's compassionate hand reaching out to us, even in our fallen state. When everyone might see us as "too deep in sin" or "too far gone" or "you have crossed the line," the Psalmist reminds us, "The LORD is near to all who call on him, to all who call on him in truth. He fulfills the desires of those who fear him; he hears their cry and saves them" (Psalm 145:18-19 NIV).

God sees deep into our hearts. As a matter of fact, Jesus identifies with our weaknesses and temptations, and he empathizes with us (Hebrews 4:15). That means he sees our struggles and wants to rescue us. I think of an animal rescuer who has to reach up to great heights or dark pits to rescue animals who cannot help themselves. They are stuck. But that animal rescuer won't leave that animal out there to perish in the dark or cold. Similarly, God wants to reach and rescue us from every single stronghold, sin, or bondage. As we turn from our sins, God will forgive us.

Do you know Jesus is interested in the way you live? For that reason, he has made provision for us to live a victorious Christian life. He freely sacrificed his life for us so we can walk in holiness and overcome sin. Therefore, if we choose to let Christ into our lives and lay down all our plans and agendas at his feet, he will teach us his ways. This is the opportune time to look to Jesus, not at our past mistakes or people's opinions. Jesus is the one who is continuously perfecting us, not condemning us. In fact, his grace is available for us to win the battles in life. As you express your great desire to walk in God's ways, declare the following:

Declaration

I will not allow sin to dominate my heart. Through Jesus Christ, I can conquer sin and live a life of righteousness. Therefore, sin will not win; his grace is holding me now.

97

God Stepped In

Have you ever been in a situation where you went through so much emotional pain that you started to lose confidence in yourself? Then you started to hear voices condemning you—telling you that you weren't capable or skilled enough to be anything good. For a while, you believed those voices. You carried those thoughts with you. Then like a mighty Warrior, God stepped in.

God loves to fight for his children. "He will not let your foot slip—he who watches over you will not slumber" (Psalm 121:3 NIV). At one point in my life, God had to reassure me that he was watching over all that was going on in my life. Because God cares about all the inhibitions, uprisings, and discomfort in our spirit, he reminded me that he wouldn't let me down. God encouraged and ministered to me, letting me know he was with me and that I could take refuge in him. So, I quietly waited on God. Then one day God told me I needed to have a new perspective, a new mentality. I needed to start thinking positively about myself. I knew it was time for me to get out. Yes, we need to get out from whatever is holding us back or keeping us trapped. Deciding to get out is the first step toward the solution. Obedience is the next.

I decided that I would obey whatever God was telling me to do, so step by step God showed me the way. I'm so thankful that as the years rolled by, God used many people—family, teachers, professors—the local church, sermons, worship, my profession, of course the Word of God, and many other facets to teach me this valuable lesson: with God, we have potential, ability, and confidence. God is the one who equips us with positive qualities. He will cause us to rise, not to sink in the mess.

Looking back, I clearly remember that one of the stories God used to minister to me was the one about Joseph's own brothers throwing him in the pit. Afterward, they sold him to Midianite traders, so Joseph found himself in a strange land (Genesis 37:24–28, 36). In Egypt, I'm sure Joseph missed his family and longed to hear the comforting words of his father. To make matters worse, Joseph was wrongfully thrown in prison, but he still stayed true to his faith in God (Genesis 39:1–21).

Many years later, Joseph obtained a huge and recognized promotion. He ended up in the palace, second-in-command of the entire land of Egypt, so Joseph became a prosperous man with a great family (Genesis 41:43–45). Wow! That's just like God to step in and help the oppressed. It doesn't matter the circumstances; God will intervene and save us with his strong arm (Isaiah 59:16). At the right time, God came through for Joseph.

I love a happy ending. This had to be God's doing: Joseph was promoted from pit to palace.

Although I wasn't literally thrown into a pit or prison like Joseph, I felt that negative emotions and condemning voices had imprisoned me. But God "lifted me out of the pit of despair ... and steadied me as I walked along. He has [even] given me a new song to sing" (Psalm 40:1–3). Actually, God lifted me out from a state of depression. Beyond the shadow of a doubt, I know God has given me a *new song to sing*; I choose to sing of the goodness and faithfulness of God. Now I know what God's delivering power looks like; the chains of self-condemnation and guilt are broken, and my soul is set free. God loves to perfect all the flaws, weaknesses, and shortcomings in our lives. So let's never give up when the going gets tough.

Currently, do you find yourself in a painful or uncomfortable situation, where it seems like there is no solution? According to Isaiah 53:3 (ESV), Jesus is "a man of sorrows and acquainted with grief." So he will personally connect to the frustration we are going through. In fact, "he is familiar with pain" (Isaiah 53:3 NIV). This means he is right there with you in your pain and struggles, waiting to help you and walk you through. Yes, he's with us during those down moments. His plan is never to keep us feeling depressed, powerless, and incompetent, but he wants to bring us out. These are the moments when the Lord himself will steady us with his hand; with his powerful arm, he will make us strong (Psalm 89:21). As you start to praise God, tell him the following:

Praise Moment

Thank you, Lord, for your hand on my life. As always, you have showed me that you will never forsake me. Like what happened to Joseph, thank you for supporting and advocating for me. Because of your faithfulness and kindness, you have brought me out of depression, which could have stifled and even stopped your plan for my life. Even now, I praise you for what you will do for me—and for others. You have good plans for our future.

98

The Weak Are Made Strong

Don't be afraid, for I am with you. Don't be discouraged,
for I am your God. I will strengthen you and help you.
I will hold you up with my victorious right hand.
—Isaiah 41:10

We don't need to carry the label that says, "I am not good
enough" or "There is no way I can overcome this obstacle,
or achieve that goal" or "Because of bad circumstances in
the past, I will never be able to rise up!" Wow! These are
appalling mindsets. They will most definitely smother our
growth spiritually and emotionally.

What kind of battles do you face on a day-to-day basis?
Are you bottling up your emotions and hiding how you really
feel about yourself? Are you making sure no one is seeing the
real you? Eventually, everything changes when someone tells
you the complete opposite of what you are feeling and thinking
about yourself.

One Bible character, Gideon, wasn't feeling good about
himself. Then an "angel of the Lord appeared to him and said,
'Mighty hero, the Lord is with you! ... Go with the strength
you have, and rescue Israel from the Midianites. I am sending
you!'" (Judges 6:12, 14).

At first Gideon didn't see himself as being capable of doing this task. "How can I rescue Israel? My clan is the weakest in the whole tribe of Manasseh, and I am the least in my entire family!" he protested (Judges 6:15). Woo! What a negative view he had of himself! Although he saw himself as not being qualified, God still referred to him as "a mighty hero." Isn't this mind blowing? Very often, the negative thoughts we have of ourselves aren't real. They are just an illusion. It's what we have created in our minds. Note: although Gideon had a poor self-image, God still singled him out as the perfect candidate for the task.

God wanted to use Gideon. Earlier the Lord let him know that he would give him the strength to rescue the Midianites. Here was the moment for him to say, "God, use me! I am available." Instead, Gideon doubted God's Word, even though the Spirit of the Lord had already clothed Gideon with power. Why did Gideon continue to think negatively about himself, when God had already equipped him with the ability and strength to do the task? Gideon lacked courage. He was unsure of himself. For that reason, he even asked the Lord for a sign, so he put out two fleece, which both proved that the Lord would use him to rescue Israel (Judges 6:36–40).

In Judges 7, we see that Gideon finally decided to take up the challenge. But there were too many men in the army. And God didn't want to use a huge army in this battle; he didn't want the warriors to boast that they had saved themselves by their own strength (Judges 7:2). As it turned out, with only three hundred men, God used Gideon to gain a great victory over the Midianites (v. 22). Wow! God showed himself strong, even with such a little army.

Although Gideon saw himself as the weakest and least important, God saw him as "a mighty hero." Through Gideon we see that God can empower even the weakest person with strength and ability. I'm glad God didn't condemn Gideon for doubting him. He still used him mightily despite his mistrust and fear, which is a clear indication that God was showing him amazing mercy and kindness. He manifested his power through him in such a remarkable way.

Do you believe God wants to use you and even to change your negative mindset? Maybe at one point of your life, you didn't think you were capable or qualified enough to do a task God was asking you to do. However, this is the perfect time to bring your vulnerability to God and see what he will do in your life.

Do you realize God wants to help and strengthen you in those areas of weakness? The Lord isn't a far-away God in those difficult and uncertain times. He is right there with us. From now onward, tell yourself, "My old self has been crucified with Christ. It is no longer I who live, but *Christ lives in me*" (Galatians 2:20, emphasis added). Yes, our old selves have been crucified. We don't need to think the way Gideon was thinking at first. He viewed himself as a weakling, whom God couldn't use. Now, because Christ lives in us, we are equipped with new strength and abilities. As we bring our vulnerability to God, he will work mightily in our lives. Through him, we cannot be defeated. Even now, declare the following:

Declaration

Lord, I declare that the Holy Spirit has equipped me with power and strength to help me in this hour of weakness. Therefore, I depend on you to help me conquer every battle that comes my way. Because you are invincible in battle and live inside me, I am now confident that I will win.

99

With Praise, Conquer Negative Emotions

You have turned for me my mourning into dancing. You have put off my sackcloth and clothed with gladness.
—Psalm 30:11 (NKJV).

Because life consists of the good, the bad, and the ugly, there are times when we need to deal with disappointments, unfairness, frustration, rejection, anger, and many other negative emotions. Thank goodness, God cares a whole lot about all the stuff we need to deal with on a day-to-day basis. God takes note of everything that's on our minds, so he knows all about the struggles we encounter and how they can affect us.

Is there a situation weighing heavily on your mind that is preventing you from praising God? Then these are the very moments when we need to turn to God. Searching YouTube and finding songs that tell you who God is, how much he loves us, and what he wants to do for us is a great way to deal with negative emotions. A few songs that come to mind are "Love So Great" by Hillsong Worship, "Goodness of God" by Jenn Johnson, and "See a Victory" by Elevation Worship. As you listen to these songs, you will come to an understanding that there is no limitation as to the way God wants to work on our behalf. He definitely wants to pour good things into our lives.

Another way we can let praise rise from our hearts is by reading the Word of God. I particularly like to read psalms of praise and adoration to the Lord. Through Psalm 31:19, 21 (NKJV), you can tell God, "Oh, how great is Your goodness, Which You have laid up for those who fear You, Which You have prepared for those who trust in You ... Blessed be the Lord, For He has shown me His marvelous kindness in a strong city!" This psalm assures us of the good things God has in store for us. This is the beauty of our God; we can count on him to show us his marvelous kindness amid trouble and disappointments.

Throughout the years, God has been teaching me how powerful praise is. In those unpredictable and wild moments when there seem to be no answers and everything is seemingly going in the wrong direction, I love to read a psalm. The writer in this particular psalm reminds us that "weeping may endure for a night, but joy comes in the morning" (Psalm 30:5 NKJV). Wow! This means we don't need to stay in our pain and sadness. God has promised to turn our weeping to joy. In faith, let's sing and be joyful, because the Lord loves to comfort his people in their affliction and suffering. God does see when we are in pain, but singing praises will change our mood. In the midst of sadness or distress, God will encourage and strengthen us. Then we will experience joy and peace of mind that "comes in the morning."

On one occasion, standing in my kitchen, I found myself crouching under the weight of many stressful things going on in my life at the time. As soon as I became conscious of this, I immediately decided I was going to put on my "dancing shoes" and get into my "praise garments." So, right in that kitchen with no one around, I did exactly that. Dancing mixed with praise completely changed my mood. As we start to acknowledge God's goodness, the celebration in our hearts will be restored, and praise will replace the gloominess, worry, and agitation.

Praise changes our posture. Instead of hanging our heads or slouching our shoulders, we can stand tall, knowing Jesus has promised to carry our heavy burdens for us. Isn't it freeing to know that as we lean on him, he will give us rest and peace of mind. Our heavenly Father is a compassionate God, who is personally interested in all our affairs. This means we can rely on him to comfort us, help us, see us through, and make a way when there seems to be no way. Instead of thinking about the negative situations or the people who can rub you the wrong way, in the meanwhile, just sing your heart out to the Lord. This is the moment for God to put a new song in your heart and fill your mouth with praise. Then watch how God will work.

Do you believe God is thinking precious thoughts about you? Will this truth about God change your perspective about how you deal with all the negative stuff going on in your life? Why not join the writer of Psalm 147:1, 3 by proclaiming, "How good to sing praises to our God! How delightful and how fitting! ... *He heals the brokenhearted* and bandages their wounds" (emphasis added)? As we sing praises to God, I believe healing will start to take place in our hearts. Even now, believe that God is about to change your sadness and mourning into joy and peace. Let's start praising.

Praise Moment

Today I will sing a new song to you, Lord. Thank you for thinking precious thoughts about me. Because you are faithful, good, and kind, I entrust you with all the circumstances that want to weigh me down. From now onward, I won't allow discouragement and complaining to take over my life. Instead, I will praise my way through, knowing you are advocating for me.

100

The Dawning of a New Day

In an instant, bad circumstances can hit us and change the course of our lives in a drastic way, as seen in Ruth's story in the book of Ruth. In the first chapter, we meet Naomi, who was in a state of brokenness. First, her husband died; then after ten years, both of her sons died. Naomi was left with only her two Moabite daughters-in-law, Orpah and Ruth (Ruth 1:3–4). As you would expect, Naomi had many questions; she couldn't understand why the Lord had brought such huge tragedies in her life.

Do you sometimes feel that the Lord has brought misfortunate situations in your life? Have these caused you to become bitter toward God? Naomi was in such a state. Her whole demeanor and language spelled blame. At the peak of her sorrow and disappointment, somehow Naomi lost her vision of who God really was. To her, life was a total mess—filled with many broken pieces, which seemed unrepairable. I am sure she must have wondered whether God would ever change her circumstances and bring joy back into her life.

Her daughters-in-law were also in the middle of this crisis. While Orpah chose to continue to live in Moab, Ruth made a bold decision to go back with her mother-in-law to live in her homeland, Judah. Ruth realized Naomi was financially and emotionally broken. Plus, she had no other son to give her in marriage. Yet as a single woman with no good prospects of the future, Ruth still told Naomi, "Wherever you go, I will go ... your God will be my God" (Ruth 1:16). What a commitment in the midst of what seemed like a hopeless situation!

It's refreshing to know that Ruth came face-to-face with the God of Naomi. She didn't want to go back to the gods of her ancestors; she wanted to serve the true and living God. We can deduce that she envisioned a God who would see them through, so she looked beyond the dark circumstances.

In chapter 2, we see Ruth didn't stay in the house and wallow in self-pity and sorrow. *She got up!* And this is what changes the whole dynamic of the circumstances. With no resources, Ruth ventured out, working in the field of Boaz. To the naked eye and to others in that field, it must have appeared that she was a woman in a destitute condition, who was gathering leftovers to get a decent meal. Little did they realize *a new day would soon be dawning!* God was the one who was orchestrating all the events in Ruth's life.

At this point of Ruth's life, nothing seemed glamorous or hopeful. But she still had something positive going for her. God had seen Ruth's true heart. Her boldness, submissive attitude, and high expectancy in Jehovah God were all making room for God to work on her behalf.

Working diligently in a field that belonged to this rich man, Boaz, Ruth had no idea he was her close relative. But as soon as Boaz realized who Ruth was, he encouraged her by saying, "May the Lord, the God of Israel, under whose wings you have come to take refuge, reward you fully for what you have done" (Ruth 2:12). Ruth learned to take refuge under the wings of her God. Isn't this what makes the difference in this scenario? Like Ruth, when we choose to look to God in the chaos, pain, or uncertain and hopeless situations, things don't remain the same. God rewards us.

Just as Boaz showed kindness to Ruth in this challenging moment, *God wants to show up in our lives* and reveal his goodness to us in ways beyond our imaginations. This is the moment when we need to carefully listen to all God's commands and follow them.

First, Ruth obeyed Boaz's command and continued to work in his field. Then she followed Naomi's instruction to go to the threshing floor and uncover his feet. There Ruth told Boaz, "Spread the corner of your covering over me, for you are my family redeemer" (Ruth 3:9). Note: Ruth went to the threshing floor on the grounds that Boaz was their family redeemer. Naomi had already observed that Boaz showed Ruth exceptional favor during the barley and wheat harvests when she had worked alongside the other women in his fields (Ruth 2:19–13), so she had a hunch that a love affair might be blooming.

At the threshing floor, although Boaz was surprised to find Ruth at his feet, his response to her was filled with grace and kindness. He saw Ruth as a virtuous woman who could have gone after a younger man, yet she chose him (Ruth 3:10). But this was the moment when Boaz had to tell Ruth about the conflict at hand. There was another man who was more closely related to Ruth than Boaz, so he was more eligible to purchase the land from Naomi and marry Ruth. Aware of this fact, Boaz told Ruth, "Don't worry about a thing, my daughter. I will do what is necessary" (Ruth 3:11–12). Doesn't this moment remind you of God's deep concern for us? In those moments when doubt and fear of the future overwhelm us, we need to hear God's voice say, "I will do what is necessary."

In chapter 4, we see this closer relative of Ruth isn't the one who redeemed Ruth. He wanted only to purchase Naomi's land, not to marry Ruth. Thank goodness Boaz did the complete opposite. He didn't see Ruth in dark, impoverished circumstances or as someone insignificant, but he purposely chose to pour his love on her and to redeem her.

Wow, doesn't Boaz's attitude toward Ruth remind you of the story of the prodigal son in Luke 15:11–24 (KJV)? The prodigal's father didn't reject his son despite his mistakes, tattered clothes, or ungroomed personality, but he showed him unconditional love. Can you imagine how that son must have felt when his father, filled with love and compassion, ran toward him, embraced him, and kissed him? Boaz did something similar. He accepted Ruth for who she was. He chose to marry her despite her background or circumstances.

After Ruth became Boaz's wife, she became pregnant and gave birth to a son. This was a pivotal moment—not only for Ruth but also for Naomi. Before, Naomi had been bitter and distraught, but God showed her he could turn any bad situation around. Instead of blaming God, she "took the baby and cuddled him to her breast. And she cared for him as if he were her own" (Ruth 4:16). Wow! God does break through for us.

Through this story, we see there were many hurdles in Ruth's path that could have dampened her spirit and caused her to worry. But Ruth teaches us a beautiful lesson about taking refuge in almighty God by being submissive, bold, and tenacious.

Like Naomi, are you facing a situation that seems impossible for God to turn around? Because of Ruth's commitment to her, Naomi reaped the benefits of the goodness of God. What a breakthrough Naomi experienced! I can picture her shouting and singing praises to God. God indeed can change the brokenness, pain, and anxieties in our lives and fill us with joy. Restoration is God's deepest delight.

Prayer

Lord, I bring all the broken pieces of my life to you. Every scar, complaint, and disobedience, I surrender to you. Let your healing power flow and make all things new and beautiful. Fill my life with a new praise—a new song—a new love for you. Amen.

Printed in the United States
by Baker & Taylor Publisher Services